FASHIONABLE FIRST LADY

The Victorian Wardrobe
of Mary Lincoln

Donna D. McCreary

To Joe Sanders
Best Wishes
Donna d McCreary

Lincoln Presentations

ISBN-10: 0-9795383-0-0
ISBN-13: 978-0-9795353-0-8

Dust jacket by Karen J. Kennedy, Design in Bloom, Indianapolis, IN designinbloom.com

Interior and text design by Sheila Samson, WordCrafter, Inc., Carmel, IN (editsheila@indy.rr.com)

To Donna and Valerie,
and of course,
to Mary.

Contents

Introduction

Mary Lincoln always enjoyed fashion. As a member of the aristocratic Todd family, she was able to adhere to the latest fashions made from the finest fabrics. The young woman was also one of the belles in Lexington, Kentucky, and in Springfield, Illinois, then a bustling frontier town. She was a member of the social plane where ladies were concerned about the width of their ribbons, the length of their skirts, and the latest Parisian fashions.

In an era when garments were made entirely by hand, much of Mary's time was occupied with sewing. In an early letter written when she was in Missouri visiting her cousin Ann, she wrote to her friend Mercy Levering: "I have scarce a leisure moment to call my own, for several weeks this fall a formidable supply of *sewing*, necessary to winter comfort, engaged our constant attention."[i] Family legends of the young Miss Todd include stories about costumes made from sheer embroidered pink muslin, layers of white organdy, leghorn hats, and feathered headdresses. These were elegant garments worn by women of the elite social set.

Like her peers, Mary gleaned the latest issues of ladies' magazines for advice on her wardrobe. In addition to the latest Parisian fashion plates, these periodicals included cooking instructions, information about raising children, advice about managing household servants, and the rules of social etiquette. To the Victorian eye, first appearance and the way one was dressed made a lasting impression, and proper ladies of that era wanted very much to leave a positive lasting first impression. Women paid attention to the details of their attire and their accessories, for one mistake could lead to social ostracism. As one French author wrote:

Those who do not wish to be taken as belonging to the vulgar, prefer to risk a wetting rather than be looked upon as pedestrians in the street, for an umbrella is a sure sign that one possesses no carriage.[ii]

And no one wanted to be considered "vulgar."

Not only did Mary wear fashionable garments, she also liked to purchase them for members of her family. When her half-sister Emily came to visit the Springfield relatives, Mary gave her a white bonnet. Emily was so pleased with the gift that she wore it when posing for a photograph. When Mary was First Lady — a term she never used and that historians argue over whether even the press used it when referring to her — Mary lavished gifts of clothing and jewelry on her sisters, nieces, and cousins. In her later years, her letters are filled with descriptions of items that she purchased for her granddaughter, her daughter-in-law, and other family members.

Even in widowhood, Mary kept abreast of the latest fashions. In 1869, while traveling in Europe, she wrote to her daughter-in-law, Mary Eunice Harlan Lincoln, directing her to take some of the best dresses, which were stored away in her trunks in her Chicago home, and use them. She wrote of a white crêpe shawl and a muslin dress with narrow flounces and encouraged the younger woman to "have this made over for yourself — in Europe — those dresses are so much worn."[iii] Mary also asked her to use the white paisley shawl, an ermine cape, velvet cloaks, camel-hair dress shawls, and countless laces.

Never having a daughter of her own, and now having a daughter-in-law and a granddaughter, Mary showered them with gifts while she traveled abroad. In France, Mary purchased a white hat; from Italy came a set of malachite jewelry. Other gifts included a lovely apple-green and white silk dress, a green silk walking suit, a striped blue and white foulard costume, evening dresses, a brown shawl, and many other fashionable items. She also sent gifts for her daughter-in-law's mother, and two parasols were sent to the baby's nurse, to be used when walking little Miss Lincoln. Precious and expensive gifts for the child — also named Mary but affectionately called "Mamie" — included dresses, caps, baby shawls, baby bonnets, an embroidered cloak, shoes, and exquisite pieces of jewelry.

Along with these gifts, Mary also offered fashion advice. She explained what colors were popular, what styles of dresses were fashionable, and what type of jewelry should be worn. Robert Lincoln, however, was concerned about the cost of everything his mother was purchasing. From the tone of one of Mary's letters, his wife must have also expressed her concerns.

> Robert writes that you were quite frightened, about the baby clothes — Certainly they were made of the simplest materials & if they were a little trimmed there was certainly nothing out of the way — the *baby* is *not* supposed to be able to walk out in the street this winter & being carried in a nurse's arms, certainly a simple embroidered cloak — is not too much, for people in *our station* of life — The very *middle classes* in Europe, dress their children quite as much & as I do not consider ourselves in that category, I would not care what the MEAN & ENVIOUS, would say.[iv]

Mary Lincoln not only enjoyed shopping — and much has been written about that — for her, it was almost an art form. She sought the best items, bargained for the best prices, and demanded the best customer service. However, although her shopping habits are heavily documented, other than purchases she made during the White House renovation, little can be found about what she bought for herself.

A few of Mary's costumes have become famous because she wore them for photo sittings, and some are known because they have been displayed in museums. While a handful of historians have commented about Mary's love of floral headdresses or her love of beautiful clothing, most do not examine how her dress style related to the fashion of the era. Did she dress like other Washington society women? Were her dresses outstanding because they were different and more elaborate than everyone else's?

Mary did dress in the latest fashions of her day. Her costumes could be found on the pages of *Godey's Lady's Book*[v] and other fashion publications. She did not create new standards, but rather was the perfect model for what was considered fashionable. As a member of the aristocratic Todd family, and then the wife of the President of the United States, Mary had a social station to maintain, which included an obligation to dress impeccably.

We know much about her wardrobe, but what can we discover about the woman by examining it?

Technical Notes

Photographic numbers: The numbers assigned to the photographs of Mary Lincoln are the ones established by Lincoln historian Lloyd Ostendorf.

Use of the word "costume": Victorian fashion books frequently refer to a lady's "costume." It is the appropriate term for one's attire.

Engravings, portraits, and other art forms are not used in this manuscript unless it is believed they were created from actual photographs of Mary.

The Victorian Wardrobe of Mary Lincoln

In Their Sunday Best

On Sundays in the early nineteenth century, the women attending church services dressed in their finest attire. Soft sounds of rustling lace, swishing batiste, printed muslin, and chintz whispered through the sanctuary as they moved among the aisles. The church pews were as colorful as a bowl of jelly bean candies as the ladies sat adorned in their garments of pink, azure blue, myrtle green, jonquil, and marshmallow.

These were the dresses of the romantic era. Fashionable bodices had high waists, wide shoulder lines, and larger upper sleeves. Skirts were ankle-length and gently pleated. The lower hem was often trimmed with one or two flounces, a padded roll at the hem, or other three-dimensional decoration.

Hats were enormous. Decorated with "flowers, immensely wide ribbons, and huge feathers," it was said that "dogs barked and horses shied at them in the streets."[1]

Little girls looked at these latest fashions and longed to be older, so they could wear them and be fashionable as well. One little girl of Lexington, who with her family attended McChord's Presbyterian Church, became frantic for one of these newest fashions. Her name was Mary Ann Todd.

When Mary was about ten years of age, her stepmother's niece, Elizabeth Humphreys, came to live with the Todd family. Slightly older than Mary, the two girls shared a bedroom and quickly became good friends. Years later, when writing memories of their youth, Elizabeth wrote that as young girls they were "dressed in the most unbecoming styles, with long sleeved check aprons for weekdays, and a little something better for church and Sunday School."[2] These "aprons" would have been worn over a chemise with two tie closures in the back — one at the neckline and one slightly lower forming an empire style waistline. The skirts were long and narrow. Their better dresses for Sunday school were distinctively children's clothing made in the same fashion but of a slightly better fabric than their weekday clothes. Mary wanted something that was more fashionable — more grown-up.

At this time in fashion history, women would often baste small reeds on the inside of their skirts. These were the same types of reeds that milliners used in drawn silk bonnets. Done properly, the effect was quite pretty, balancing the wide shoulder and sleeves, and it also kept the skirt from wrapping around a woman's legs.

Mary wanted one of these "hooped" skirts. According to her stepcousin Elizabeth, Mary knew that if she asked for one, her request would be denied. How to obtain one caused her great worry until, "at last she hit upon an expedient."[3]

Mary's plan was to visit a neighbor, Mrs. Hostetter, one Saturday afternoon, and ask her for some of the branches from her weeping willow tree. She and Elizabeth could then sew the branches into their dresses and wear them to Sunday school the next morning. Elizabeth agreed to the plan. "So at the convenient time, she [Mary] put on her pink sunbonnet, took a basket and went off. It was a long time before she came back, but she was supplied abundantly with the needed article. We were afraid to begin our preparations until after tea. Then we took a light, went up stairs and locked the door. Seated on the floor we lost no time in the important work before us, but we made poor progress."[4]

Both of the girls were startled when Mrs. Todd came to the door and told them to put out their light. Of course, they obeyed her and put out the candle. The girls then sat quietly in the dark until enough time had passed that they thought everyone else in the house was asleep. They relit the candle and sewed until a late hour. According to Elizabeth:

> When we hung up the finished garments with a thrill of delight, our sleep was too short to be refreshing. We managed to get to breakfast in time and as soon as it was over rushed to our room. Mary was always quick in her movements, but just then she made uncommon haste and was dressed and out on the street as I reached the front door of the hall. One moment and we would

have been safe, but as fate would have it, Aunt caught a glimpse of me. One glance was enough to show what we had been up to. She reached the door in a second and called Mary back, and there we stood before her, a burlesque on vanity, two of the most grotesque figures her eyes ever fell upon in hoops that bulged in front and at the back, while they fell in at the sides with our narrow white dresses stretched over them to their utmost extent. We had basted the willows in just as they came off the tree, one end being very large and the other being very small. [Mrs. Todd] looked us over from head to foot, and said what frights you are. Take those things off and then go to Sunday school. We went to our room chagrined and angry. Mary burst into tears and gave the finest exhibition of temper I have ever seen or known her to make. She thought we were badly treated, and expressed herself freely on the subject. I was angry too and said quietly to myself as much as she had uttered.

It was well our display was confined to our own premises. If we had got into the McChord church which we were so anxious to do, the congregation would have been convulsed with laughter and [Mrs. Todd] too much mortified to lift up her head.[5]

Mary's disappointment was appeased when her father returned from a business trip to New Orleans. He brought with him several yards of lovely sheer embroidered pink muslin — enough for both girls to each have a new frock. For the first time, Mary was allowed to determine the fashion of her own clothing. She supervised the details of the dress and made sure that the "sewing woman" (one of the Todd family slaves) followed her every detail. [6]

This fastidious attention to fashion details remained with her throughout her life. Years later, her older sister Frances stated that she was "one of the best seamstresses I ever knew. She made all her clothes and her children's clothes; and they were better made than most anyone else's."[7] Mary's skill as a seamstress and her love of fashion made her wardrobe spectacular. She was one of the better dressed ladies in

Springfield. As the President's wife, her taste in fashion was both admired and criticized by members of Washington society and members of the press who thought her clothing too extravagant for times of war.

Simple Frock
June 1828

When Robert Smith Todd married his second wife, Elizabeth "Betsey" Humphreys, Mary gained a new family. The Humphreys were an aristocratic family from Frankfort, Kentucky. Their matriarch was Betsey's mother, Mrs. Alexander Humphreys. Grandmother Humphreys held a special place in Mary's heart. She was a highly educated woman who read and spoke French. She was an "exquisite in dress and mind and manner, the quintessence of all elegance, virtue, and culture which Mary hoped to emulate."[8]

One day in late June 1828, Mary and her stepcousin Elizabeth were to visit Grandmother Humphreys for an entire week. It would take nearly four hours to travel the twenty-six miles along the Frankfort Pike to their final destination. Wearing dainty slippers and white organdy frocks with blue satin sashes, the two girls climbed the three folding steps of the Todd carriage to begin their journey. Their faces were protected from the summer's sun and heat by wide-brimmed leghorn hats trimmed with pink roses.[9] These dresses were the white ones the girls also wore to Sunday school. The dress skirt was gathered into the slightly raised waistline and flared gently out toward the ankles. A chemise, or underdress, was also worn. It would be several years before Mary and Elizabeth would wear full dresses.

Evening Dress
Late 1839

When twenty-one-year-old Mary Todd moved to Springfield, Illinois, she heard many stories about Abraham Lincoln, the junior law partner of her cousin, John Todd Stuart. In late 1839, Mary finally met this rising frontier lawyer and politician whom had been the subject of many discussions.

Some historians accept that the couple met at "the grand cotillion in honor of the completion of the new [Illinois] capital building"[10] while family legend says the party was held at the home of Mary's sister, Mrs. Ninian Edwards. Where the couple met may be debatable; it is certain that they two were intrigued with one another. After being introduced to Mary, Mr. Lincoln said to her, "Miss Todd, I want to dance with you the worst way." Afterwards, Mary told her cousin, Elizabeth Todd, "And he certainly did."[11]

They shared only the one dance that night, for when Lincoln started toward Mary again that evening, she held out her dance card to reveal that it was filled with names of young men who were waiting to dance with her.

The dress she wore that evening was described as billowing masses of lace and organdy, all pink and white in color. Mary's skirts swayed to the waltz music revealing little glimpses of her pink satin slippers and matching silk stockings.[12]

Soon after the dance, Abraham and Mary were often found reading poetry together on the sofa at the Edwards' home.

White Skirt
1842

A broken engagement, a rushed wedding ceremony, a simple engraved gold band, a nervous bride and groom, family objections, and spilled coffee are all elements of the Lincoln wedding stories and legends.

Elizabeth Edwards was against the marriage. As the eldest sister and Mary's guardian, she felt a responsibility to help her young sibling find a suitable husband. Thus, with the assistance of their sister Frances and other Todd relatives, Mary was introduced to many of the eligible bachelors of Springfield. One of the most prominent beaus was Stephen A. Douglas. However, Mary was most interested in the "rough diamond" from Kentucky, Abraham Lincoln.

Elizabeth did not deem Abraham Lincoln a worthy suitor for her younger sister nor did she hesitate to voice her opinions. She enlisted the support of other Todd family members in Springfield who were all too eager to offer their advice and objections to the relationship. Lincoln was on a different social plane from the Todds. His family "had not yet struggled up from the dirt and puncheon floors," whereas Mary's family lived in homes where the floors were "waxed and polished like mirrors."[13]

Although the Todd clan found Lincoln to be "honorable, able, and popular, his future they said, was nebulous. His education had been desultory. He had no culture, he was ignorant of social forms and customs, he was indifferent to social position."[14]

Despite family objections, Abraham Lincoln and Mary Todd were married on November 4, 1842. The couple had met in secret for several months and did not tell Mary's family of their plans until the day of the wedding. The family legend claims that Elizabeth was so rushed to prepare for the ceremony that the wedding cake was still warm when the bride and groom sliced it.

Years later, when asked what the bride had worn, most guests

White Skirt, 1842. (Photo courtesy of Abraham Lincoln Presidential Library & Museum [ALPLM], Springfield, Illinois. Photo by Jim Helm.)

agreed she wore a "white muslin dress." One different recollection is that Mary wore a white silk brocade skirt currently on display at the Abraham Lincoln Presidential Museum, reported to be the same skirt that her sister Frances had worn as a bride a few years before. Family legend explains that Mrs. Frances Patterson, a granddaughter to Frances Wallace, had inherited this skirt from her grandmother. Since Mary and Abraham had little time to plan their own wedding, Mary borrowed her sister's dress, which unfortunately was subjected to a coffee spill during their reception.[15] The skirt on display does have a couple of stains on it which appear to have been caused by some sort of "spill," but this is not enough evidence to confirm the family story. Plus, one wedding guest, Mrs. Mary Edwards Brown, claimed Mary spilled coffee on the bodice of her dress, not the skirt.[16]

In an 1895 interview, Frances told a newspaper reporter that Mary did not wear this skirt for it was too soiled. Along the hemline, there is a large brown stain which appears to be dirt. If this skirt was stained as such when Mary wed, then it was indeed too dirty to be worn for such a special occasion. Frances stated that Mary "may have been married in a white swiss muslin."[17] She went on to say that she was not sure if Mary even wore a white dress (which was not mandatory for weddings in that day and age) and questioned whether or not the dress was made of muslin stating, "I think it was delaine, or something of that kind."[18] However, two other wedding guests both stated that Mary did indeed marry wearing a white muslin gown. Mrs. Benjamin Edwards, the sister-in-law to Ninian Edwards, reported that Mary wore a white muslin dress. Katherine Helm, using a recollection from Elizabeth Todd Grimsley, stated "the bride wore one of her lovely embroidered white muslin dresses."[19]

Whether or not Mary wore this skirt as her wedding dress may never be known. However, we do know that she wore this white silk brocade skirt while she and Abraham Lincoln were courting. According to Frances, this skirt had belonged to her and was the one she wore at her own wedding to William Wallace, and that Mary "never had a white silk dress in her life till she went to Washington to live."

She went on to say that after she gave Mary the white satin dress, she "told her to wear it till it got soiled, but then to give it back to me, for I wanted to keep all things like that — my wedding dress, you know."[20]

The skirt consists of six panels of twenty-inch-wide material. The waistline is gathered, more fully at the back. It is somewhat longer in back than in front with slightly gored panels to give more fullness at the hem. The skirt is made of a silk brocatelle fabric which has a small floral pattern. The bodice has been lost over the years. (Location: ALPL, Springfield, Illinois.)

Striped Dress
1846

Several photographers visited Springfield in the 1840s. It is believed Abraham and Mary Lincoln visited one of the temporary studios of photographer N. H. Shepherd. Most historians agree that this daguerreotype was made between June and December of 1846.[21] If the likeness was taken before her birthday on December thirteenth, Mary would have been twenty-seven years old when photographed. The Lincolns had companion exposures taken — one individual pose of each of them. According to Robert Todd Lincoln, the original daguerreotypes hung on walls in the Lincoln's Springfield home.[22]

For her photograph, Mary probably chose to wear one of her more fashionable dresses. In the mid-1840s, "there was a marked taste for materials with horizontal stripes"[23] and Mary's fabric choice depicts that taste. The "round dress" was fashionable, and skirts were worn very full. Sometimes as much as seven widths of fabric (fifteen to thirty inches wide) would be used in a skirt with no flounces. This style of skirt was sometimes decorated with "rows of ornamental buttons, running down the whole length in the center of the dress."[24] The photo shows two rows of large, ornamental buttons on Mary's skirt. The large ones in center

11

Striped Dress, 1846. (Reproduction photo, author's collection; identified as ML, O-1)

front appear to be shaped somewhat like sunflowers. The companion buttons in a row to the right side of the skirt also appear floral in design. Most likely, a third row of the smaller floral buttons, not visible in the photograph, was on the skirt's left side. A more appealing visual effect would have been achieved by having more than two rows of buttons.

The bodice has a wide neckline to visually balance the width at the hem of the skirt, and it has a traditional hook-and-eye back closure. Sleeves remained very tight in the mid-1840s, cut on the bias and slightly gathered at the elbow to permit movement. Mary's sleeves have a dropped shoulder line and are fashionably tight fitted, finished with white ruffles at the wrists. Separate cuffs or ruffles could easily be removed and washed, and would save wear on the edges of the fashion fabric of the dress. Silk, like this dress, would generally not be washed. The waist of the dress is low and pointed at the center front. Mary wears a ribbon cincture at the waist.

A sheer, elbow-length, lace-trimmed bertha, pulled close at the neckline with a brooch, compliments Mary's ensemble.

Lavender Summer Dress
Early 1850s

As a child in Springfield, Emily Huntington (later Mrs. John Todd Stuart, Jr.) lived across the street from Mary's sister, Elizabeth Edwards. In her 1918 memoirs, Emily wrote of watching Mrs. Lincoln walking home after visiting Elizabeth: "She had on [*sic*] beautiful summer lavender dress with a long train and I distinctly remember to this day with what fascination I watched her train swish from side to side, leaving a long serpentine trail behind her. Fashions were different then, and feet and legs were not in evidence as they are now."[25]

A description of Mary's dress does not exist, but walking across town she would have worn a day dress with a high bodice and a skirt made full by layers of petticoats. Summer fashions were often made of a lighter weight fabric such as cotton, gauze, or lightweight muslin. The most popular fabric choice for ladies was light-weight silk.

Even in the summer heat, a lady was expected to wear an outer garment such as a mantle or shawl over her dress. Lace mantles were popular for warmer climates. Their purpose was to protect the fashion fabric of the lady's dress.

Miss Huntington's memory of Mary's costume brings credence to the humorist of the nineteenth century who often poked fun at women's fashions. It was said that "trailing skirts gave rise to the story that the municipal authorities found it an unnecessary expense to employ street cleaners for doing what ladies so kindly performed gratis."[26] Despite jokes and ridicule of the style, women still wore the fashion of the day.

⚜

Lavender Winter Dress 1854–1855

By December of 1854, there were four Todd sisters living in Springfield: Elizabeth (Mrs. Ninian Edwards), Frances (Mrs. William Wallace), Mary (Mrs. Abraham Lincoln), and Ann (Mrs. C. M. Smith). It was the winter party season, and Springfield ladies were busy donning their newest creations to wear to the many parties, dinners, and balls that were held. The Todd sisters were also quite busy making plans for a visit from a younger half-sister, Emily Todd. "Little Sister," as Lincoln had dubbed her, was now eighteen years old and was coming to Springfield for an extended visit of six months.

Emily noted that during her visit, Elizabeth Edwards and her sister-in-law, Mrs. Ben Edwards both entertained several times.[27] She does not give much description of Mary's gowns, but commented, "I was struck with her exquisite taste in dress."[28]

Mary's excellent skills as a seamstress were put to use that winter. Emily remembered that Mary had made one gown that was "a lovely lavender brocade, and which she wore with a round point lace collar."[29] She does not say if this was a day or evening style dress.

In the 1850s for day wear, a boned, high bodice with a long waist line would be worn. The pagoda sleeve had come into vogue, and fancy undersleeves were worn under the pagoda. Basic fashion required a day bodice to be made separately from a skirt. Both the bodice and the skirt were fully lined with white cotton or glazed silesia. Many women made a day bodice and an evening bodice to interchange with one skirt. [30]

In 1853, the report from Paris was "skirts become wider and wider."[31] The skirt width at the hem had become so large that instead of gathering the skirt at the waist, deep pleating was the most common manner of forming the waistline. Layers of petticoats were worn to achieve the desired width. A day skirt often was adorned with three to five flounces.

Evening wear included a low, tight bodice with a deep point. Short sleeves were fashionable and were covered with a lace bertha.

An evening silk skirt would have either three broad, or five or seven narrow flounces which were "almost always a disposition."[32] Stiff petticoats were worn in the evening and often had three or four rolls to support the width of the skirt. The skirt was said to have a "graceful fan-shape."[33]

Floral Evening Dress
1855

By 1855, an evening costume was usually made with a tight-fitting, low corsage and short puffed sleeves which were concealed under a bertha. The bertha was described as often being made of "tulle or blonde (silk lace) folded and crossing in front."[34] The effect of the bertha was graceful and light over the tightly fitted and boned bodice and the ever widening skirt. Three, five, or seven flounces often trimmed with ruching or ribbons were found on fashionable skirts. Some dresses boasted rows of puffed tulle which alternated with rows of flounces.[35]

Elizabeth Edwards held a dinner party and invited the Todd clan on several occasions during Emily's visit. One such family gathering was an incentive for Mary to make a new dress. Emily described it as "a white silk with blue brocaded flowers scattered over it in bunches and little garlands."[36]

When Lincoln arrived home from his law office, Mary was already dressed. She gently reminded him that he too needed to change his attire for the party. According to Helm:

> He looked at her with a smile and said, "Fine feathers enough on you to make fine birds of both of us." Noticing her dress still further, he said, "Those posies on your dress are the color of your eyes." Mary dimpled with pleasure. "You see, Emily, I am training my husband to see color. I do not think he knew pink from blue when I married him."[37]

Yellow Dinner Dress
Circa 1855 or 1856

One observer commented that "If ladies' dresses continue to increase in breadth, it will be absolutely necessary to widen all the public thoroughfares. Perhaps it is the spirit of exclusiveness which has induced the leaders of fashion to surround themselves with barriers of barége and other similar outworks to keep the common herd at arm's length — or rather at petticoats' breadth." [38] It is certain that as skirts widened and dress trims became more elaborate, the cost of a fashionable lady's wardrobe increased. Every lady of status was properly attired for social functions. Not only was her costume scrutinized by members of her community, so were her manners and the conduct of her entire family.

Mary Lincoln loved social affairs. As a belle in Springfield, she had often been the center of social attention. As a matron, and the wife of a former U.S. Congressman, Mary continued to enjoy an active social life.

Miss Ardelia "Delie" Wheelock, a teenage neighbor, recalled one hectic evening as the Lincolns prepared to attend a grand affair at the home of Mr. and Mrs. Jesse Dubois who lived just a few blocks from the Lincolns on Eighth Street.

Ladies often needed assistance in donning the layers of starched and flounced petticoats required to achieve the popular fan-shaped skirts. One observer stated, "Many belles now wear fourteen [petticoats] in evening dress. They go to a ball standing up in their carriages and stand between the dances, for fear of crushing their dress and fourteen petticoats." [39] Corsets laced in back; bodices closed in back. If a woman did not have a daughter, servant, or maid to assist her with her toilet, she often had a young girl from her neighborhood assist. Delie Wheelock was a favorite of Mary's, and no doubt she enjoyed helping Mary arrange her finery. She recalled Mary's dress was a "lovely canary colored satin with a low neck and short sleeves." [40]

As Mary and Abraham were dressing to attend the reception, Willie and Tad Lincoln came home from a taffy pull. The remnants of sticky molasses candy covered both of the boys. When they saw their mother and father were getting ready for a party, they wanted to attend too. Mary firmly explained the party was only for adults, and they could stay home with their brother Robert. As the boys began to protest, Mary repeated that they could not attend the party. This raised an onset of howls, kicks, and screams.

Mr. Lincoln intervened on the boys' behalf and it was agreed the boys would go with their parents, staying in the kitchen while their parents attended the party. Mr. Lincoln stated he would take the boys in through the back way thus avoiding the reception itself.

Miss Wheelock and Robert cleaned and dressed the boys in such a haste that Tad's trousers were put on him hind-side front. Little boys' knee breeches were often cut loose for comfort and durability. Since they buttoned to the shirt on all sides, the front and back of the garment were very similar. As Tad, who was three or four years old, cried that "he could not walk good," Lincoln waved his hand and reminded little Tad that he had to behave.

Once at the Dubois home, Willie and Tad both managed to leave the kitchen and mingle with the guests at the reception much to Mary's chagrin and Lincoln's amusement. Since the reception was intended for adults only, most of the guests would not have been amused that children were in attendance. The editor of *Godey's Lady's Book*, Sarah Hale, had written that "If you are a mother, the crowning grace of your household management will be that you have rightly trained the children committed to your care."[41] Seeing the Lincoln boys at such an elaborate event would have caused any adult in attendance to wonder about any other shortcomings of Mary's household.

Brown Day Dress
Circa 1857 or 1858

This brown silk day dress is attributed to Mary Lincoln and is part of the Van Cortland collection.

The bodice of this dress has a front hook-and-eye closure with eight ornamental cloth-covered buttons down the center front. The bodice measures fourteen inches in length from the neckline to the waist. The armscye is slightly dropped as was fashionable at this time. The upper arm of the sleeve has some fullness, but it becomes tighter below the elbow. The sleeve cuffs fit tight at the wrist; finger points extend down the back of the hand. Bretelles come to a point at the waist center front, across the shoulders, and come to a point at the waist center back. Bretelles became a popular bodice trim in Europe during the mid-1850s. By 1857, fashionable dresses often had a "cape à la bertha, or bretelles as capes, fringed."[42] American fashions were not far behind those in Europe. Both the sleeve cuffs and bretelles are trimmed with fringe. In addition an unusual row of fringe runs horizontally across the bodice between the bretelles. The back of the bodice is trimmed in the same manner as the front.

The skirt consists of eight panels with pleating in the back of the skirt only. The skirt measures thirty-seven and three-fourths inches from the waist to the hemline.

This costume was completed with a matching headdress and a parasol. This costume is an excellent example of fashionable attire for a lady at home even if it was not owned or worn by Mary Lincoln. (Location: National First Ladies' Library and Museum, Canton, Ohio.)

Brown Day Dress, circa 1857 or 1858. (Photograph courtesy of the National First Ladies' Library.)

Silk Double Skirt with Mantle
1860

Fashion had changed considerably for women during the past five years. Layers of petticoats were uncomfortable for women. Multiple layers of petticoats were not only heavy, they were also hot to the wearer and made it difficult to walk by tangling the legs. To ease this problem, the crinoline was invented in 1856. This undergarment was "an open cage of metal hoops graduated in circumference and held at intervals by vertical tapes attached to a waistband, which allowed for skirts of even greater width at the hem, as well as increased comfort for the wearer."[43] It allowed a woman's limbs to be free of the confining petticoats and allowed air to circulate under her skirt. In wintertime, not so much air circulation was desired, and many women chose to wear a warm underpetticoat or flannel drawers for insulation.

The crinoline also created new problems for a woman. If the wearer sat down incorrectly, the crinoline would tilt up. If she stood too close to a piece of furniture, it would tilt back. It swayed from side to side while she walked. Walkways became congested with the width of the crinoline. A hostess had to add more seating when entertaining, for sofas that had held two or three guests comfortably in the mid-1850s, now held only one lady and her crinoline. The dangers involved in wearing a crinoline included entanglement in carriage wheels and the fear of being blown off of one's feet during a strong wind. However, the greatest threat to a woman's life was the danger of fire. Light-weight fabrics, especially tulle and muslin, worn in evening attire were most flammable. Homes could be heated only by open fires or iron stoves, which could quickly ignite fabric inadvertently touching it. If a woman's clothing were to catch fire, she could not be rolled in a carpet to extinguish the flames because the crinoline still allowed air to flow. People throughout the world were shocked when they read of the catastrophe at the Cathedral in Santiago, Chile, in early December 1863. More than two thousand women were burnt to death as the vast quantities of fabric fed the flames.[44]

Silk Double Skirt with Mantle, 1860. (Photo courtesy of The Lincoln Museum, Fort Wayne, IN [Reference #3155])

In 1860, America elected Abraham Lincoln as President. Because the public wanted to know something about Mrs. Lincoln and the boys, Mary and her two youngest sons posed for a photograph at the studio of Preston Butler in Springfield. Since this was the public's first image of Mary, it is most likely that she chose to wear her best dress, bonnet, and mantle (a loose, cape like garment). It is possible the photo was slightly rushed in the activity after the election. The trio does not appear to be posed at all. They simply stand in front of the camera with a simple painted backdrop and no props. Willie is looking in another direction.

In this photograph, Mary wears a silk double skirt with two deep flounces. The geometric pattern consists of small and large diamond shapes as well as a horizontal strip. The fabric's design is printed "en disposition," and was manufactured specifically to be used as flounces. The bodice of the dress is not visible, but white undersleeves can be seen under the dark-colored mantle, which is trimmed with elaborate ribbons. She wears a white-lace-trimmed collar which was probably fastened with a brooch. Her bonnet is trimmed with lace, flowers, and leaves. The bonnet ribbons are two-toned and coordinate with the ribbons on her mantle. Dark wrist length gloves complete the ensemble. It is not difficult to imagine Mary gathering her sons to leave the studio and returning to the sidewalk, clearing a wide path with her hooped skirt.

Oak-colored Silk with Gray Leaves January 1861

After the election of 1860, a vast number of packages began to arrive at the Lincoln's home. As Lincoln pulled a very elegant new hat out of he box, he said to Mary, "Well, wife, there is one thing likely to come out of this scrape, anyhow. We are going to have some new clothes!"[45] As a member of the aristocratic Todd family, Mary *knew* that new clothes were in order for the entire family. On January 10, 1861, Mary and her brother-in-law, Mr. C. M. Smith (her sister Ann's husband) and the Hon. Amos Tuck of New Hampshire went to New York to begin making purchases for the White House and for suitable wardrobes for the family to wear in Washington City.[46]

They arrived in New York on January 12. As Mary shopped in the New York stores, she was followed by reporters who wanted to see the new Madam President. One reporter commented on Mary's attire during her excursion by writing, "Her dress was a brown or oak-colored silk, with grayish flowers and leaves. It was made full, with flounces fitted well, hung gracefully about her person, and trailed just a trifle. Her bonnet was of black silk, trimmed with cherry ribbon, which, with a dark mixed shawl, neatly fitted kid gloves, and a rich lavender-colored parasol, completed her costume."[47]

From the written description, it is possible that this is the same mantle and bonnet that were worn in the photograph in November 1860.

White Moiré Silk
February 6, 1861

In addition to shopping for new household items and clothing in New York City, Mary had many things to do to prepare for the family's departure to Washington City. The house had to be rented. Furniture had to stored or sold. While cleaning out her house, Mary burned many of her personal items including old letters and old photographs. Treasured items were given to friends and family members, and a new home had to be found for all of the family pets, including that loveable forty-pound, yellow-brown dog of questionable ancestry, Fido.

But most importantly, Mary had to find time to plan her first official levee (a formal reception to honor someone) before leaving Springfield. Friends and family wanted to help the Lincolns celebrate their new position, and the Lincolns wanted to thank all of the people who had helped achieve success. A newspaper reporter from the *Missouri Democrat* described the evening by writing:

> Mr. Lincoln threw open his house for a general reception of all the people who felt disposed to give him and his lady a parting call. The levee lasted from seven until twelve o'clock in the evening, and the house was thronged by thousands up to the latest hour. Mr. Lincoln received guests as they entered and were made known. They then passed on and were introduced to Mrs. Lincoln who stood near the center of the parlor and who I must say acquitted herself most gracefully and admirably. She was dressed plainly but richly. She wore a beautiful full train, white moiré-antique silk, with a small French lace collar. Her neck was ornamented with a string of pearls. Her head dress was a simple and delicate vine arranged with much taste. She displayed but little jewelry and this was well and appropriately adjusted. She is a lady of fine figure and accomplished address and is well calculated to grace and do honor at the White House.[48]

Mary's trip to New York was a success.

Dark Silk
February 13, 1861

On the morning of February 11, 1861, Abraham Lincoln, his eldest son Robert, and a few other men boarded a train in Springfield bound for Indianapolis, Indiana. At the suggestion of General Scott, for security purposes, Mary and her party took a later train that evening with plans to join Lincoln at his destination. Traveling with Mary were her sister Elizabeth Edwards; Elizabeth's two daughters; Mary's cousin, Elizabeth Todd Grimsley; and the two younger boys, Willie and Tad.[49]

Upon arrival in Indianapolis, Lincoln and his friends were met at the train station by Indiana's governor, Oliver P. Morton and a thirty-four-gun salute. That evening, a dinner and reception was held in Lincoln's honor where he reportedly shook the hands of over three thousand well-wishers.

The next day, Lincoln and his party arrived at the train station to find that the Indianapolis and Cincinnati Railroad management had decorated the train with U.S. flags and red-white-and-blue bunting. During most of the trip, the engine pulled only two cars. However, during some segments, more cars were added for local dignitaries to travel a small portion of the journey. One car was reserved exclusively for the Lincoln family.

The train station was jammed with people who wanted to bid farewell and good luck to the President-elect. Lincoln did not make any speech or give any parting words at the station. He quickly stepped up into the car and was greeted by his family. On schedule, Mary and the boys had arrived about eleven A.M. Willie and Tad leaped upon their father with youth and exuberance. And it was said, "As they climbed into his great arms, he stopped and kissed their blue-eyed, brown-haired mother, and his own deep-set eyes went moist."[50] With the family intact again, the entourage continued their journey.

Along the way, many of the cities and towns were bedecked with flags and other festive decorations. People were seen shouting and waving flags as the train made its way from city to city. At every stop, people gathered in hopes of catching a glimpse of the President-elect and his family. The train schedule allowed the Lincolns to spend the evenings in larger cities where receptions and dinners were held in their honor. The first of these that Mary attended was in Columbus, the capital of Ohio.

The evening of February 13, 1861, an evening reception was held at the governor's residence. Guests included state officials, members of the legislation, the city council, members of the press, and special guests. No doubt, members of the Republican political party who had helped bring

Lincoln to victory were in attendance. Their candidate had won, and this was their opportunity to meet the man and shake his hand.

It was customary for men to gather in one parlor where they were known to drink hard liquor, smoke cigars, and discuss politics. Ladies were to be sheltered from such manly behaviors and would therefore gather in another parlor where they could discuss more feminine issues and enjoy their own refreshments. After meeting Lincoln in one parlor, the guests were ushered to another parlor. There, with the assistance of the governor's wife, Mary received her guests. It was reported that Mary wore a "very rich, dark-figured silk with headdress to match."[51]

The scrutinizing of Mary's wardrobe by the press was just beginning.

Steel Brocade
February 20, 1861

The Presidential party traveled toward Washington City at approximately thirty miles per hour stopping, along the way. Although he often appeared at the back of the train as it was ready to depart a station, he made few speeches during this trip. Since the press could not say anything about his words, they made note of his appearance. It was reported that his overcoat was thin and worn-looking and atop his head sat a weather-beaten plug hat. When the party arrived in Buffalo, New York, on February 18, 1861, Mary asked William Johnson, an attendant to the party, to bring forth a couple of items from the baggage car. William returned with a handsome broadcloth overcoat and a hat box. Most likely these were items Mary had purchased during her January trip to New York City. The press reported that they improved Lincoln's appearance by 50 percent.[52]

At the Astor House in New York City, Mary held an evening reception on February 20, 1861. She entered the reception parlor with Mrs. Hamlin, the wife of the vice-President-elect. There Mary was introduced to a roomful of guests. She then took the arm of Mr. James Watson Webb, who escorted her into the ladies' parlor. Mary was accompanied by her sister, Mrs. Elizabeth Edwards, and Mrs. Webb. The five hundred guests in attendance found Mary attired in a stylish gown which had been a purchase from her January shopping trip to New York. The newspapers reported Mrs. Lincoln costume consisted of

> . . . a steel brocade robe, trimmed with box quilling [a type of ruffle] of ribbon edged with lace, which extended from the waist to the lower part of the skirt where it ended in a neat gathered bow. Flowing sleeves with point lace undersleeves, added to the pleasing arrangement of her dress. A neat point lace collar secured by a fine diamond brooch encircled her neck. She wore diamond earrings to match. Her headdress was of chenille and gold. She also carried a small ivory fan.[53]

Blue Silk
March 4, 1861

Lincoln had warned a friend of his, "Don't let your wife come to my inauguration. It is best for our women to remain indoors on that day as the bullets may be flying."[54] Before Lincoln was inaugurated, the leadership of the Confederate States of America was already in place and Jefferson Davis had been elected and inaugurated as President. The Confederate flag was flying in seven states, including Virginia, just across the Potomac River from Washington City. There had been threats of assassination against Lincoln's life. The air was filled with fear and anticipation while the streets were filled with spectators and soldiers. Under these circumstances, Lincoln appeared on the inaugural platform at the Capitol Building. There he was sworn in as the sixteenth President of the United States, clad in a plain black broadcloth suit that had been given to him by Titsworth & Brothers of Chicago for the occasion.[55] Mary, her sons, Mrs. Grimsley, and other Todd family relatives occupied the diplomatic gallery.[56]

That evening, Washington society would glean their first impressions of Mary Lincoln as she attended her first Inaugural Ball. Newspapers reported that the guests, totaling up to three thousand people, began to arrive at the event around nine P.M.[57] They were first ushered to the nearby City Hall where the Council Chambers and Committee Chambers were used as dressing rooms.[58] Dirty streets, lack of climate control, and cramped carriages made travel for women inconvenient even in the best of circumstances. The expansive hoops and delicate fabrics required for evening wear made it quite impractical. It was customary to wear a carriage dress to an event, and then change into an evening costume after arrival.

The inaugural hall, dubbed by the press the "Palace of Aladdin," had been erected especially for the evening's festivities and conveniently connected with the city hall.[59] Soldiers surrounded the parallelogram shaped hall which was draped with red and white muslin. The walls were decorated with "numerous shields ornamented with our national arms." The Marine Band filled the hall with lively music, and the mood of the room was light. As one newspaper reported, "To judge by the youth, beauty, brilliancy, fashion, and hilarity everywhere predominant, no one would have imagined that a cloud was in our national heaven."[60]

The presidential party arrived sometime around eleven P.M. President Lincoln entered the room with Vice President Hannibal Hamlin and Senator Henry Anthony of Rhode Island. It was customary for the President to enter with fellow politicians, and for Madame President to enter on the arm of another man. *The New York Times* reported, "Behind the President came a couple, the sight of whom was singular and yet eminently gratifying. Singular, because so wholly unexpected and gratifying, because it was an indication of the beginning of an era of good feeling."[61] Everyone was surprised to see Mary Lincoln enter the room escorted by Senator Stephen A. Douglas from Illinois. He had competed against Lincoln for the Presidency and lost. Years early, he had competed against Lincoln for the hand of Miss Mary Todd, and lost.

While all of the women who attended this gala event were undoubtedly beautifully costumed, Mary did not disappoint those waiting to see her spectacular gown. Mrs. Lincoln was superbly dressed in a low-necked, blue watered silk trimmed with Alençon lace and a blue ostrich feather in her hair which was exceedingly becoming. Her ornaments were pearl, and *Frank Leslie's Illustrated Newspaper* noted that Mary had camellias in her hair.[62] Mrs. E. F. Ellett wrote, "All eyes were turned on Mrs. Lincoln, whose exquisite toilet and admirable ease and grace, won compliments from thousands.[63] According to *The New York Times*, ". . . her attire such as commended itself to the good taste, the sense of propriety, and the love of the beautiful of every person in the room. Mrs. L. was evidently a lady of refinement, of tact and of taste."[64]

Once again, Mary was the belle of the ball.

Tiffany Seed-pearl Parure 1861

The six-piece seed-pearl parure consisting of a necklace, earrings, pair of bracelets, and a brooch was a favorite of Mary's. She wore it to the inaugural ball in 1861 and wore either selected pieces or the entire set in several photographs. Newspaper accounts mention pieces of the parure worn with various costumes throughout the years the Lincolns occupied the White House. The set was considered so beautiful and unique that after Mary wore the parure to the inaugural ball, a prominent Washington jeweler, M. W. Galt & Bro., made copies of the set to sell in his own store.[65]

President-elect Lincoln had purchased the parure for his wife from Tiffany and Company of New York City at the "then-impressive price of $530 — more than his weekly salary as President."[66] During the inaugural trip to Washington, the Lincolns arrived in New York on February nineteenth and spent the entire next day visiting the city and meeting some of the political leaders and most famous merchants. It is believed Lincoln purchased this set at that time. Tiffany's seed-pearl pieces were exquisite and lavish because they used various sizes and more pearls per square inch than other jewelers. Their jewels were clearly the most suitable choice for the new Mrs. President.

Mary's parure was a matching set. Her bracelets were made differently from many sets of the era. "In place of the usual strands of pearls connecting the rosettes, the bracelet bands were made of articulated plaques of gold with a continuous engraved stripe of rococo ornament running through the middle."[67] There were three oval medallions of pearls on each bracelet, the one in the center being larger than the others. Each of these is decorated with matched pearls. Her earrings are double looped and match the medallions on the bracelets. The brooch was made of the same design as the bracelets.

The necklace belonging to this set of jewels consisted of one large center medallion and a center pendant. Four medium medallions and thirteen smaller were used to make the necklace. "Small gold blossoms separate the graduated oval pearly bosses."[68]

There are some questions about Mary's necklace. Photographic images show that every piece in this set had the same medallion design. Currently, the matching necklace and pair of bracelets are located in the Library of Congress; the location of the earrings and brooch are unknown. However, in photographs of Mary wearing the floral evening gown (ML, O-9 and ML, O-11) the necklace is slightly different in style: the medallions are more circular than the ones found on the other pieces. Could it have been replaced by the necklace with the oval medallions? Could it be a similar necklace belonging to a different parure? Or perhaps it was one of the copies made by M. W. Galt & Bro.? It is impossible to know why Mary wore this different necklace. It is obvious from other photographs and engravings that she wore the oval necklace more often.

Cashmere Wrapper
March 5, 1861

As Madame President, Mary had a schedule filled with receptions, levees, and state dinners. Fine fashionable attire was required for each event, and according to the custom of the era, different styles of costume were required for different events and times of day. A lady of society with a full social agenda was required to change her garment as many as five times in one day. In order to dress appropriately, one of Mary's first responsibilities was to hire a talented dressmaker. After her arrival in Washington City she inquired to several of her lady friends to recommend a dressmaker who could fulfill the needs of her wardrobe and the needs of her visiting female relatives as well.

Elizabeth "Lizzie" Keckley had been born a slave. Through hard work, and with a superb talent for dressmaking, she was able to earn enough money to purchase her own freedom and the freedom of her son. By 1860, she was one of the most desired dressmakers in Washington, but it was her goal to sew for an occupant of the White House. Mrs. General McClean recommended the seamstress's services to Mary, arranging for the two women to meet at Willard's Hotel on inauguration day.[69] Mary was understandable busy at the time and made arrangements for Lizzie to meet with her at the White House the next morning at eight A.M. When Lizzie arrived, she found three more mantua-makers who had been recommended for the position waiting for interviews. Mary spoke with all four women, but only Elizabeth Keckley was able to satisfy Mary's personal requirements.

When Mrs. Keckley came to the White House on that first morning, she found Mary "dressed in cashmere wrapper, quilted down the front; and she wore a simple headdress."[70] *Godey's Lady's Book* depicted many styles of wrappers including one which resembles the one described by Lizzie. A quilted skirt, quilted tablier (front panel), or both were most appropriate and fashionable for winter months. Made from warmer fabrics such as cashmere, the wearer was provided with layers of warmth.

A wrapper was a loose-fitting garment worn by women of all social levels when they were at home. It resembled a loose or unfitted day dress since it preserved the same fashionably shaped high bodice, pagoda or bishop sleeve, and armscye which sat low on the shoulder. It could be tied at the waist, buttoned down the front, or belted, and some had a set of drawstrings at the waist to add more fit. These gowns were often worn without a hooped petticoat for additional convenience, and for comfort some women wore them without a steel-boned corset and with a more flexible foundation garment.

It is not possible to identify all of the dresses Lizzie Keckley made while employed by Mary Lincoln. Mary had traveled to New York and purchased many new gowns prior to moving to Washington. Throughout her years in Washington, she continued to travel and purchase both gowns and dress making supplies. Lizzie reported that during the first few months after the Lincolns moved to Washington, she "made fifteen or sixteen dresses for her (Mary) during the spring and early part of the summer."[71]

Antique Rose Watered Silk
March 8, 1861

Mary's choice of dress for the first White House reception was an antique rose colored, moiré silk gown. Lizzie measured Mary for the dress and assembled it in her shop. When she returned the next day to fit the dress, Mary made a few suggestions concerning alterations in style. The seamstress later recalled: "Mrs. L looked elegant in her rose-colored, moiré antique. She wore a pearl necklace, pearl earrings, pearl bracelets, and red roses in her hair." Even Mr. Lincoln noticed Mary's lovely attire when he commented, "I declare you look charming in that dress. Mrs. Keckley has met with great success."[72]

By now, skirts had reached their maximum circumference and began to flatten in the front. More of the skirt moved towards the rear, sometimes in a train for fancy dress. Even though still nearly a decade away, the bustle was in its infancy. One Parisian fashion journalist wrote: "All the robes continue to be spread out like fans. Observe I say fans, *not* bells; the bell-shaped is now absurd."[73] Skirts were often trimmed only on the lower portion, emphasizing the width of the skirt.

Flounces still appeared on evening costumes, but they were narrower than in previous years, especially in thin materials such as silk or tulle. Moiré or watered silk was one of the most popular fabrics of choice. Evening wear for 1861 was influenced by an important chemical innovation made from a by-product of burning coal. In 1856, the first aniline dye was developed, which produced the color mauve. The colors alizarin and indigo were soon to follow. In 1860, aniline dyes were developed in the colors of magenta and solferino. In England, magenta was used for "dresses, petticoats, bonnets, and stocking, as well as ribbons; it was described as the queen of colors."[74]

Magenta Gown
March 12, 1861

On March 13, 1861, an article in *The New York Herald* stated:

> Mrs. L. was attired in a rich Magenta colored brocade silk, with raised figure flounces, trimmed not extravagantly with rich point lace. Her ornaments were chiefly diamonds and pearls.[75]

Some historians believe this to be the same dress worn at the reception on March 8, 1861. However, there are differences in the dress descriptions and the accessories worn by Mary. The difference in fabrics, one being a moiré antique and the other being a brocade silk, demonstrate that these are clearly not the same gown. Mary wore this rich magenta silk gown at the party held at the White House on March 12 in which there was music and dancing.[76]

Lilac Organdy March 1861

Julia Taft was the older sister of Tad and Willie's playmates Bud and Holly Taft, and the daughter of Judge Horatio N. Taft, the chief of the U.S. Patent Office. She often accompanied her brothers on their visits to the White House where she would read quietly or converse with Mary. She recalled how Mary would ask her questions and encourage her to express her opinions, something that was not usually allowed in the presence of elders.

A few days after the boys' first visit to the White House, Julia, Bud, and Holly returned for another day of fun and frolic. Mary placed Julia beside her on the sofa and began a friendship with the sixteen-year-old young girl. (Mary had always hoped for a daughter of her own.) Julia remembered that Mary was dressed "in a fresh lilac organdy and looked very attractive."[77] Nothing else is known of this robe, but most likely it was a lovely morning dress, or wrapper intended to be worn at home.

Julia also recalled how Mary was very particular about her wardrobe. As Madame President, Mary was expected to dress like Republican royalty. It was her position that caused newspaper reporters to record details of her attire, her jewelry, and her manner. Other Presidential wives had led the fashion scene for Washington society, and Mary had every reason to believe she would do the same.

It was with this expectation that Mary and Julia's mother had an exchange involving bonnets. Mrs. Mary Taft had purchased a new bonnet from Willian, a prestigious, fashionable milliner with a shop located on Pennsylvania Avenue. For Mrs. Taft, he had made a delicate straw bonnet that was "lavishly trimmed with purple ribbon embroidered with small black figures. It had long strings which tied with a bow under the chin." On a Wednesday afternoon, Mrs. Taft and Julia attend a concert given by the Marine Band; they played at the White House every Wednesday. Mrs. Taft wore "the bonnet, together with a purple and white silk over a moderate crinoline, and lavender kid gloves." At the close of the concert, she and Julia went up to the south front, where the Presidential party was sitting. Mary took Mrs. Taft aside to speak with her and explained that Willian had made her a bonnet with the same ribbon but did not have enough for the strings, and Mary wanted her strings to match the other ribbon on her bonnet.

An agreement was made between the two women and the milliner. Mrs. Taft gave up her strings, and Willian retrimmed her bonnet with lavender white-embroidered ribbon instead of purple. Both women seemed pleased with the exchange. Mary received the bonnet ribbons she wanted, and Mrs. Taft had a more beautiful bonnet than at first.

Not long after the incident, Julia reported to her mother, "Mrs. Lincoln wore a purple dress and those strings which were on your bonnet at first." Mrs. Taft quickly and sharply reproved her daughter. "Never let me hear you make any remark about Mrs. Lincoln's clothes, Julia. The wife of the President should be above petty gossip."[78]

Sadly, neither the rest of Washington society nor the press agreed with Mrs. Taft.

Blue Silk Evening Dress, March 1861. (Photograph courtesy of the National First Ladies' Library.)

Blue Silk Evening Dress
March 1861

Research indicates that this two-piece aqua silk evening gown was purchased during the Old Clothes Sale in New York in 1867. The inscription, "Mrs. A. Lincoln March, 1861" is written on the skirt's waistband. It is believed Mary either wore or purchased this gown at that time. The dress has been altered (at least taken in and shortened) so its exact original style is impossible to determine.

The dainty bodice has a pointed center front and small short sleeves trimmed with blue velvet, black lace, and white lace. All of the trim appears to be original to the dress.

The skirt consists of nine panels of fabric. Pleating is visible at the waistline. A pocket is located on the right side of the skirt.

Overall, this dress is in fragile condition. There may have been original trim on the skirt which has since been removed. The color and style of the garment are similar to others Mary wore during her first year in the White House. (Location: National First Ladies' Library and Museum, Canton, Ohio.)

White Silk with Flowers
1861

Jane Grey Swisshelm was a journalist who supported the anti-slavery and women's rights movements. During the Civil War she moved to Washington to work and to volunteer in the military hospitals. While in Washington she met and befriended Mary Lincoln. After Mary's death Mrs. Swisshelm wrote a letter to the editor of the *Chicago Tribune* praising Mary and sharing a few of her recollections of Mary.

Mrs. Swisshelm had noticed Mary's attire and her "full share of the general love of personal adornment." Yet she also knew that Mary

White Silk with Flowers, 1861. (Photo courtesy of The Lincoln Museum, Fort Wayne, IN (Reference #96) [identified as ML, O-9])

"would have joined a society pledged to use no foreign dress goods, laces, or ornaments during the War, if Mr. Lincoln and his Secretary of the Treasury had not condemned the project, declaring that the Government needed the revenue coming from the importation of these luxuries. They thus made the wearing of rich clothing a patriotic duty."[79]

The dress worn in this photograph is an expression of Mary's love of personal adornment and her patriotic duty.

It is believed Mary posed for this photograph at Matthew Brady's Washington portrait gallery in 1861.[80] Four photographs (one seated pose, three standing poses) of Mary wearing this gown exist today. While some of the existing cartes de visite show the 1861 date, as with so many of Mary's photos, others show the year 1862.

Keeping with the style of the era, her evening bodice has a low décolletage. Mrs. Keckley commented that Mary "had a beautiful neck and arm, and low dresses were becoming to her."[81] The long point at the bodice waist is visible at the center front. Mostly likely, there was also a point at the center back closure. The back of the bodice would have closed with hooks and eyes and a silk cord laced through metal grommets.

In the 1860s heavier dress fabrics were more fashionable than they had been in previous decades.[82] This white silk fabric is covered with bunches of dainty flowers resembling nosegays. Small dots are scattered over the fabric. The symmetrical placement and size of the dots suggest that this dress was made from either a woven brocade or machine embroidered fabric.

Mary wears a fine point lace bertha that gossips believed to have cost around two thousand dollars. It was a separate piece that was sewn on a small ribbon or casing and placed around the neckline of the gown.

Mary's costume also included white, wrist-length gloves, a fan, and flowers. The small bouquet and headdress were made with cabbage roses. It was fashionable to trim the corsage of a bodice with lace, flowers, and other elaborate trimmings.[83] Mary received both praise and criticism for the use of flowers in her costumes. Some comments, while at first appearing to be complimentary, had a negative twist to them as well. Such is the case as one observer quoted in a Lexington, Kentucky newspaper. Mrs. C. thought that Mrs. Lincoln was "very gorgeous, she stuns me with her low-necked dresses and the flower beds which she carries on her head."[84]

In this costume, Mary also wears one of her favorite sets of jewelry, the Tiffany seed-pearl parure.

This dress pattern has been mistakenly identified by historians as a Dolly Varden pattern.[85] "Dolly Varden," a fictional character created by Charles Dickens, was known for wearing bright-colored clothing, especially cherry red. Many items of fashion have been named after this character, including a printed fashion fabric, a style of dress, and a large hat. The "Dolly Varden" printed floral fabric was not manufactured until 1866. The style of dress became popular during the early 1870s and the hat was popular during the Edwardian era. None of these items were available at the time of Mary's photograph.

Day Dress
Circa Spring or Summer 1861

This likeness of Mary is a finely engraved portrait, most likely done from a photograph. The original photograph has never been found although numerous copies of the engraving still exist. It was the custom of some engravers to destroy the photographs they used for their artistic endeavors. Apparently, that was the practice of William Sartain of Philadelphia who created this likeness.

Even though there is not a date on the engraving, fashion plates in the March 1861 issue of *Peterson's Magazine* describe this style of dress as a carriage dress. Mary's dress appears to be made of a high sheen fabric with such as satin, polished cotton, or taffeta. Although a black

Day Dress, Circa Spring or Summer, 1861. (Steel engraving, author's collection. [identified as ML, O-6])

and white engraving offers little clues as to the color of the dress, the most fashionable colors for the season included Havannah (between cinnamon and olive brown), green, mauve, and violet blue.

The bodice is typical of those made for day dresses during this era. It is a high bodice with a front closure. Bodices were usually lined with a white fabric such as muslin, or a crisp, brown-glazed fabric, or even remnants of calico from other projects. Bones about six inches in length were sewn into the bodice sides and smaller bones were sewn into the front. This helped give the wearer a smoother fit and helped the bodice stay in place over the corset.

The sleeves are set slightly off the shoulder. Mary's bodice shows an asymmetrical trim placed on the left shoulder, then descending diagonally to the center front at her waistline. According to period fashion plates, the same trim would generally continue along the same diagonal line down the skirt front until it was a few inches above the hemline. There, the trim was turned at a ninety-degree angle and ran diagonally until it reached the hemline. The trim was then placed around the entire circumference of the hemline.[86]

It is impossible to know if Mary's costume followed this pattern exactly, but it was fashionable to trim a bodice and a skirt in the same manner. Thus, Mary's skirt surely was trimmed to compliment the bodice. It was written that gored skirts "should be made with two whole breadths at the back; the gores formed by cutting one breadth slantwise are about three nails wide on the top."[87] (One nail is two and a half inches. Three nails is seven and a half inches.)

In 1861 women often wore either a narrow, scalloped, falling collar that was fastened with a brooch, or a narrow collar and black silk cravat. Mary has chosen a narrow white collar and either a silk cravat or a ribbon tie. She also wears a ladies' watch looped around her neck with a cord.

Vertical Striped Dress
First Half of 1861

It has been recorded that Mary posed for a photograph at Matthew Brady's studio wearing this ensemble in January 11, 1862.[88] However, the photograph must have been taken during the first six months of the Lincoln's White House stay. Mary's cousin, Elizabeth Todd Grimsley, traveled to Washington with the Lincoln family to witness the inauguration of President Lincoln. She stayed with them for the first six months of the administration and helped Mary with some of her official duties and entertaining. When Mrs. Grimsley returned to Springfield, Mary gave her this dress and a black Chantilly lace shawl that had been given to Mary by the French Ambassador. Years later, the dress and shawl were handed down to Mrs. Grimsley's descendants. One of them altered the dress by removing one or more panels from the skirt and making a new day bodice.[89]

This two-piece bodice-and-skirt ensemble is made of off-white silk taffeta woven with purple flowers and black stripes.[90] The striped pattern repeats itself with alternating plain and floral stripes. One stripe contains a small purple flower that is bell shaped. The next stripe is plain in the center. The next floral stripe contains a purple flower with six petals. The next stripe is plain, and then the pattern repeats. The photograph reveals evidence of gored skirt panels. The bodice waist has a long point at the center front. Most likely, the center back is pointed as well. The bodice has a fashionable back hook-and-eye closure. For her photograph, Mary's bodice is adorned with a lace bertha that covers the short sleeves of the bodice and the upper part of Mary's arms. Her costume also includes white wrist-length gloves and a lace handkerchief.

Mary's hand-held nosegay consists of a center gardenia and smaller flowers such as a hydrangea or sweet william. The greenery is similar to Italian ruscus.

The bouquet on the bodice front and her headdress are both based around large cabbage roses and smaller sweetheart roses. A small

Vertical Striped Dress, First Half of 1861. (Reproduction photograph, author's collection. [identified as ML, O-21])

flower such as hydrangea or sweet william is used as filler, while the same greenery used in the nosegay is also in these pieces. Although it is impossible to determine the color of the flowers used in the floral pieces, it is possible some of the smaller flowers are purple to coordinate with the purple flowers woven into the skirt pattern.

Completing the ensemble is the six-piece seed-pearl parure set created by Tiffany's of New York that Mary received as a gift from her husband in 1861. According to family members, Mary's jewelry was "not magnificent and consisting mostly of small pearls finely strung in dainty design and small diamonds set down closely in pearls (*pavé*, I think the French call it) were unusual and especially appealing to a refined and cultured taste."[91] Not only does this pearl set appeal to a refined and cultured taste, it is magnificent.

The type of floral choice and low décolletage Mary wears in this photograph caused Senator James W. Nesmith of Oregon to write to his wife:

> The weak-minded Mrs. Lincoln had her bosom on exhibition and a flower pot on her head, while there was a train of silk or satin, dragging on the floor behind her of several yards in length, as I looked at her I could not help regretting that she had degenerated from the industrious and unpretending woman that she *was* in the days when she used to cook old Abe's dinner, and milk the cows with her own hands.[92]

Senator Nesmith apparently was not a connoisseur of ladies' fashions. Perhaps Oregon's distance from the fashion center on the east coast prompted his fondness for a farm wife's wardrobe. One can only imagine how this comment was received by Mrs. Nesmith! (Location: Smithsonian Institution, National Museum of American History, Division of Politics and Reform, First Ladies Collection, Washington, D.C.)

White Silk with Ruffles
First Half of 1861

For critics who thought that Mrs. Lincoln had previously looked as if she had a flower pot on her head, in this photo she gave them reason to think she also had a rose bush attached to her bosom. Fashion advisors in that year suggested that, for evening attire, a young woman should wear a wreath with a cache-peigne of flowers behind. It was suggested a matron wear a diadem of flowers, feathers, or gauze and gold cable cord twisted together in her hair.[93] Mary's most popular choice was the matronly crown of roses or other fresh flowers.

In this photograph Mary wears a diadem of flowers consisting of a large cabbage rose in the center and smaller roses on the side. A smaller flower, which could be hydrangeas or sweet william, is used to fill in areas of the headpiece. Instead of a small bouquet at the center front bodice, Mary wears a garland of flowers which begins at the center front of the bodice, extends diagonally to the left, and continues onto the skirt to slightly below her left knee. The garland is made primarily of rosebuds and also includes flowers at each end that appear to be the size and shape of a dogwood blossom. The dark green leaves appear to be something such as Italian ruscus. These offer a contrast for the colorful flowers against the white fabric of the gown.

Mary's gown is a two-piece evening dress made of white silk. The bodice has a fashionable, low, off-the-shoulder neckline and an elongated center point at the bodice waist. There is a hook-and-eye back closure. Two ruffles made from silk fabric with small bouquets of printed flowers enhance the bodice neckline and cover the short sleeves. Each sleeve also has two ruffles made from the same floral material.

The gored skirt is made with a small train that would have swayed gently as a lady walked and dusted her floors behind her. Mary's choice of a white dress indicates this dress was worn primarily for a receiving line and perhaps a grand march in the carpeted East Room of the White House. The bottom of the skirt is decorated with five rows of three-inch

White Silk with Ruffles,
First Half of 1861. (*Above*:
Reproduction photograph,
author's collection [identified as
ML, O-13]. *Right*: Reproduction
photograph, author's collection.
[identified as ML, O-19].)

ruffles made from the same floral print fabric as the bodice ruffles. Each ruffle was sewn on to a cord in a casing, gathered, and then sewn to the skirt. The bottom ruffle would have been placed on the skirt first, and following ruffles would be placed farther up the skirt until complete. The top edge of the top ruffle was covered with a white silk ribbon, or ruching, for a finished look.

In this photograph Mary's hair, diadem, and jewelry are the same as in the vertical striped dress. Close examination of this photograph, shows the nosegay that she held while wearing the vertical stripe dress, and in other photographs wearing this dress, lying on the table beside the statue. These two photographs were taken on the same day.

Blue Silk
May 9, 1861

Newspapers reported that President and Mrs. Lincoln held a brilliant White House reception for members of the military and their families. In attendance were commissioned officers and families of the Army, Navy, Marine Corps, and the volunteer militia of Washington. Mary's costume was described as "very elegant blue silk, richly embroidered, and with a long train; also point lace cape, and a full set of pearl ornaments, in which she well sustained the dignity of her station."[94]

Evening gowns of 1861 were made with gored skirt panels and demi-trained skirts. The bodice waist was always closely fitted, pointed in front and often pointed in back as well. While it is impossible to know exactly what design this dress had, certainly it was the latest fashion.

Honoré de Balzac, the nineteenth-century writer, believed a woman's attire was:

. . . a permanent revelation of her most secret thoughts. . . . Dress is a sort of symbolical language, the study of which it would be madness to neglect. To a proficient in the science, every woman walks about with a placard on which her leading qualities are advertised.[95]

During this era, *Godey's Lady's Book* and other period journals stated that a woman's home was a reflection upon her. For generations, the social scene in Washington had been ruled by members of the southern elite. Many felt that the Lincolns, being from the West, were not suited to the social climate of the nation's capitol. Rumors emerged about Mary's lack of social skills even before she arrived in Washington. Mary planned to prove them wrong. She was a highly educated member of the aristocratic Todd family who had received twelve years of formal education. Her goal was to prove to Washington society that she was a most capable hostess. And she planned to achieve this goal through her elaborate dress and beautiful home.

Over the years, the White House had become a vermin-infested, disheveled old building greatly in need of renovation. One observer at the White House commented that it looked like some "old and unsuccessful hotel."[96] Renovation became Mary's first order of business, and several shopping trips to New York were made to conduct this business. As Mary and her cousin Mrs. Grimsley ventured from store to store, a reporter from the *Philadelphia Sunday Dispatch* followed them at a distance. This reporter apparently spoke to store clerks to gain information about Mary's purchases. Some of it may have been true; other reports may have been a store keeper's attempt to promote his business. Before Mary had returned to Washington, a sarcastic article appeared reporting that Mary had purchased black point lace shawls at Stewart's for six hundred and fifty dollars each and a camel's hair cashmere shawl for one thousand dollars,[97] which were outrageously expensive items whether she actually purchased them or not. Of course, this was merely gossip as the reporter did not speak to Mary directly. But the damage to Mary's reputation had been done and every newspaper wanted information about her shopping sprees. Elizabeth Grimsley, who accompanied Mary during her trips to New York, wrote:

. . . but what was our amazement upon taking up the New York papers, after our return home to find we had been on an extensive shopping trip; that Lord & Taylor, Arnold and Constable, and A. T. Stewart had been largely patronized, that Mrs. Lincoln had bought, among other things, a three thousand dollar point lace shawl, and Mrs. Grimsley had also indulged, to the extent of one thousand, in a like purchase, (and par parenthesis, this was the nearest I ever came to having one,) whereas we had not even driven by the stores.[98]

These particular shawls may not have been purchased during this trip, but Mary did purchase many items to refurbish the White House. Bell pulls, carpets, rosewood furniture, draperies, wallpapers, and beautiful solferino trimmed china were all purchased in New York.

Maroon Striped Silk Day Dress 1861

This maroon, woven striped-silk day dress is attributed to Mary Lincoln and is part of the Van Cortland collection of First Lady artifacts.

The costume consists of an eight-panel skirt and a day bodice. A pocket is located on the right side of the skirt. The high plain bodice has dropped shoulder armscyes. The pagoda sleeves have a slight scalloped edge that is trimmed with black velvet and lace. The bodice has a front closure with ten functional black celluloid buttons, and jockeys are made from the fashion fabric. A narrow black-lace trim decorates the neckline.

Maroon was a popular color among members of the aristocracy, and a dominant color in Mary Lincoln's personal wardrobe. Even if this costume did not belong to Mary Lincoln, it still is an elegant example of

Maroon Striped Silk Day Dress, 1861. (Photograph courtesy of the National First Ladies' Library.)

the fashions worn by middle and upper class women when they were at leisure. (Location: National First Ladies' Library and Museum, Canton, Ohio.)

White Silk
August 3, 1861

Prince Napoleon Joseph Charles Paul Bonaparte of France visited Washington in August of 1861, and on the third of that month Mary entertained the prince with a dinner for forty invited guests. It was an important visit not only for the Lincoln family but for the government of the United States. Prince Napoleon was a cousin to the Emperor of France, and it was imperative that France side with the Union and not the Confederacy.

There was little said about Mary's attire at the dinner party. It was reported that she entered the state dining room on the arm of the prince and was "simply but tastefully attired in white."[99]

Julia Taft received a little fashion information from the Lincoln boys. Tad had reported that the ambassadors 'were all tied up with gold cords; they glittered grand." To which Willie added, "Pa looked pretty plain in his black suit, but Ma was dressed up, you bet."[100]

"Heavily Veiled"
August 15, 1861

Mary traveled to New York where she visited Princess Clothilde, the wife of Napoleon at a hotel. Apparently Mary wished to have some privacy during her trip, for it was reported that she was "heavily veiled."

White Grenadine
August 22, 1861

The humidity, poor sewage system, and the vast number of soldiers all added to the unpleasant smells which rose from the swamps and streets of Washington. Often, Mary traveled north to get away from the sweltering heat and vile smell of the city. In August 1861, she and a group of friends traveled to New York and then to Long Branch, New Jersey, a resort. That afternoon Mary and her traveling party, escorted by the former Governor William A. Newell, attended a demonstration of life saving equipment. In the evening, Governor Newell hosted a "grand hop" at the Mansion Home in Mary's honor. Her ball gown was described as:

> . . . an elegant robe of white grenadine, with a long flowing train, the bottom of the skirt puffed with quillings of white satin, and the arms and shoulders uncovered, save with an elegant point lace shawl. She wore a necklace and bracelets of superb pearls, a pearl fan, and a headdress of wreathed white wild roses. Beyond all comparison she was the most richly and completely dressed lady present.[101]

Ball gown trims included exquisite laces. Mary's sister Emily recalled that Mary owned but little lace, but that which she did have was of the finest quality.[102] Popular laces included Black Maltese, Black Spanish, rose point, Honiton, or English thread. Summer shawls were made of either lace or embroidered camel's-hair cashmere. A fine shawl, even one made of wool, could be pulled through a wedding ring, and a lightweight shawl was much more convenient during the heated summer months than a mantle or a cape.

Black Velvet
1861

Francis Bicknell Carpenter, the famous artist, knew the Lincoln family well. On February 6, 1864, he moved into the White House and stayed for six months. His purpose was to create a painting of Abraham Lincoln reading the Emancipation Proclamation before the Cabinet members. In November of 1865, Carpenter had another project in mind: He was making plans to paint a portrait of the Lincoln family as they had appeared when first arriving in Washington in 1861. For accuracy and inspiration for his subject, he wrote to Mary Lincoln (who was then living in Chicago) in the fall of 1865 to request photographs of family members.

On November 15, 1865, she replied, "There is an excellent painted likeness of me, at Brady's in N.Y. taken in 1861 — have you, ever seen it? I am sure you will like it & I believe, it was taken, in a black velvet."[103]

The image existing today is what Lloyd Ostendorf referred to as a "painted-over photograph." A photographer would take a dim photo of a person and then artistically improve it with hand painting. This photo shows where Mary was "slimmed" by removing part of her dress at the back and the bosom.[104]

The dress is a depiction of 1861 fashion. It features a high bodice with a front closure. Fashion advisors wrote that "any trimming which conceals the figure or heightens or widens the shoulders is in execrable

Black Velvet, 1861. (CDV author's collection [identified as ML, O-4])

taste."[105] Mary's dress follows this fashion advice. Her white cloth collar has a dainty scalloped edge and is fastened by a black brooch trimmed in pearls. Her earrings, headdress, and bracelet complete her matching jewelry. It is obvious from this photo (and from earrings currently in archives) that Mary had pierced ears.

The most fashionable dresses made from rich fabrics such as velvet had wide, open bell-shaped sleeves. Mary's pagoda sleeves are lined with white fabric and delicately trimmed with what appears to be a narrow white ruching on the inside hem edge of the sleeve. A wide, dark trim forms a cuff on the sleeve. A white lace handkerchief hangs from the waist of the dress and Mary holds a dark colored fan in this photo.

The skirt is gored; it shows the "bell" shape of the latest style of crinoline that took up less room in front of the wearer and more room behind. This allowed a greater display of fabric than the recent "round" hoops without colliding with objects or people approached by the wearer. By 1861 skirts for both day and evening wear were slightly gored at the sides. "One breadth on each side [of the skirt] is sloped two inches at the bottom; five or six pleats are set in on each side of the front and three or four box pleats behind."[106] This effect flattened the front of the skirt and made the entire garment more elliptical in shape, at the same time reducing the bulk of fabric at the waist and allowing greater fullness at the hem.

Day Dress
1861

Not much is known about this engraving of Mary. It is believed to be the work of John Sartain of Philadelphia, and is believed to have been made from an original photograph. Nothing is known of the time, place of origin, or the name of the photographer.[107]

Day Dress, 1861. (Photograph courtesy of The Lincoln Museum, Fort Wayne, Indiana. (Reference #99) [identified as ML, O-5])

Mary wears a jeweled headdress that has a bow in back. Other jewelry worn to complete the costume include drop earrings and a matching brooch. These jewels have dark centers encircled by pearls and are the same earrings and brooch as she wore in the photograph ML, O-4. Mary again wears the drop earrings in photographs ML, O-23 and ML, O-24.

Her day dress has a high plain bodice and is made of a rich fabric. It is difficult to tell in a black-and-white photograph, but the fabric appears to have a texture such as velvet. The bodice front has a long point at the center front. The fourteen buttons down the center front are ornamental buttons, for the bodice would have a hook-and-eye closure.

The sleeve seams are dropped off the shoulder as was suggested by the fashion of the day. Gathers on the sleeve are visible in the photograph. It is impossible to tell if the sleeves are pagoda or bishop in style.

Small pleats, such as cartage pleating, is visible at the center front of the skirt, and a small white collar with a scalloped edge completes the costume.

Black Silk Dress 1861

Mary Lincoln was photographed wearing this gown sometime in 1861. Existing cartes de visite have been found with the imprint of Matthew Brady's New York studio. In addition to the New York studio, Mr. Brady also maintained a portrait studio in Washington. It was a common practice to use the same negatives in both galleries; therefore, it is impossible to know if Mary sat for this portrait in Washington or New York.

This black silk charmeuse dress has a fitted bodice and gored skirt common to most dresses of the era. Both the bodice and skirt are fully lined with a soft brown, loosely woven linen or lawn fabric.

Black Silk Dress, 1861. (*Above*: Photo courtesy of the Abraham Lincoln Presidential Library and Museum, Springfield, IL. Photo by Jim Helm. *Right*: Photograph courtesy of The Lincoln Museum, Fort Wayne, IN (Reference #4523) [identified as ML, O-8])

The attached collar is made of a fine white lace. Its design is of a floral motif with leaves forming a pointed edge.

The fashionable pagoda sleeves are set into the shoulder of the bodice with a bright green narrow piping. This is most unusual for the era, as most piping was made from the same fashion fabric as the dress. The lower edges of the sleeves are trimmed with a three-inch-wide purple ribbon along the edge. Along both the top and bottom edges of the ribbon is a single row of three-fourths-inch-wide bright green ruching. Thus, only about an inch of the purple ribbon is visible. The inside of the sleeve is lined with a white cotton fabric. The inside edge of the sleeve is trimmed with one-inch wide, white ruching that gracefully comes to the edge of the sleeve hem.

The bodice closes with a hook-and-eye front. Ten buttons are sewn onto the front closure for decorative purposes. Each button, shaped like a six-petal flower, is covered in green thread with a gold thread center.

The most outstanding feature of this dress is the elaborate silk-embroidered design on the fabric. Large bunches of purple and white leaves and berries are elegantly spaced on the gown. Between the large bunches are small clusters of green leaves and red berries. The berries appear to be either strawberries or raspberries. Either would be appropriate for Mary Lincoln to have worn. She was famous in Springfield for her berry parties and continued the custom while in the White House.

Sadly, several years ago this dress was displayed in a sunlit window and is now severely damaged. The colors are faded on the right side of the dress, and in many places the fabric is cracked and fragile. The dress has been stabilized by a conservator, yet it remains too fragile for permanent display. (Location: ALPL, Springfield, Illinois.)

Silk Brocade
December 17, 1861

The first White House public reception for the social season was held on December 17, 1861. Beginning at eight o'clock in the evening, President and Mrs. Lincoln received their guests. The social custom of the era was for the President and his wife, or other female relative, to hold large public receptions where anyone could attend and meet the President. *Leslie's* described these events as "throwing open the Presidential mansion to every one high or low, gentle or ungentle, washed or unwashed who chooses to go, and the net result is always a promiscuous, horrible jam, a species of social mass-meeting."[108]

For this particular occasion, it was reported that Mrs. Lincoln was in fine spirits. Her gown was "a light figured silk brocade, elegantly flowered, and her fingers sparkled with diamonds and pearls."[109]

Two Purple Dresses
December 1861 – January 1862

On December 14, 1861, Prince Albert, the Prince Consort and husband of Queen Victoria, died of typhoid fever. Rumors flew among the gossips of Washington society claiming that Mary Lincoln intended to wear ceremonial mourning in sympathy for Queen Victoria and planned to encourage everyone else in Washington to follow her example. If true, the "Republican Court" (as it was often called in the newspapers) would have glided across the polished White House floors wearing an array of purple, lavender, or white at every event during the entire party season. With such a limited palette of colors, the trim and style of the gown would need to be exquisite in order to be noteworthy.

It is doubtful these rumors were true. Ceremonial dress was common in European courts, but not American society. It is doubtful women in the United States would feel obliged to wear mourning attire simply because the President's lady requested it. With the Civil War nearing its first full year, and the vast number of Union defeats, families were more concerned with the war efforts on the home front than they were European society. Many women were already in various stages of mourning for their own family members. To ask them to mourn the Prince Consort of England for an entire social season would have been a ridiculous request.

During this time, Mary did have two purple costumes. Julia Taft wrote, ". . . one a very regal purple velvet with white cord piping and buttons. The other was a rich silk. However, she wore a fine point lace shawl with the velvet gown and white roses in her hair, which certainly was not mourning."[110]

Purple Velvet with White Piping
December 1861 – January 1862

Perhaps the purple velvet dress with white cord piping and buttons that Julia remembered is the gown currently located at the Smithsonian Institution. Although Julia's description is somewhat vague, her description does resemble this beautifully preserved dress.

Two bodices were made to wear with this purple velvet skirt. One bodice is for day wear and the other for evening wear. It is the day bodice which Julia mentioned in her writings.

The day bodice is a fitted darted bodice, boned, and constructed with five separate panels. The bodice front joins together with a hook-and-eye front closure. Ten ornamental, square, mother-of-pearl buttons decorate the bodice front closure. The center back fits across the shoulders, then curves inward and outward again below the waist forming a somewhat

Purple Velvet with White Piping, December 1861 – January 1862.
(Photographic post card, author's collection.

hourglass shape. A nine-inch peplum extends from the center back panel. The bodice front has a four-inch center point extending below the natural waistline.

Every seam of the bodice is piped with white silk satin cording. The piping is also along the neckline and the finished edge of the bottom waist. Two long darts, located on each of the front panels, are piped with the same white satin cording. The armscyes, jockeys, and sleeve seams are piped in the same manner.

The dropped shoulder seams are hidden by jockeys made from the fashion fabric. A one-inch-wide white-silk ruched trim is located on the inside edge of the pagoda sleeve

The evening bodice is piped in the same fashion as the day bodice. The front has three vertical rows of piping which accentuate the seam lines and the long, pointed center front. The décolletage consist of a black lace bertha with white lace trim. The fine sleeve frills are made of black Chantilly lace which is set in silk pillow lace. A white machine-made net lace is used to trim the black Chantilly.[111] The evening bodice has a back closure.

The skirt, which was worn with both bodices, consists of thirteen panels of varying widths. Each panel is piped with white silk cording as is the hemline of the skirt.

Accessories for this costume include a purple silk parasol trimmed with black lace and a purple silk fan with ivory sticks. The purple silk fabric of the fan has a "purple silk edging but no decorations." The sticks have "curved shoulders and double scalloped edges near the rivet."[112] This fan consists of sixteen sticks. (Location: Smithsonian Institution, National Museum of American History, Division of Politics and Reform, First Ladies Collection, Washington, D.C.)

Dark Robe
January 1, 1862

Entertaining at the White House was always a special occasion, but the New Year's Day receptions were always extraordinary. Weeks in advance, Mary's devoted her time to overseeing the event's preparations.

Hosting public receptions had been a social responsibility of the President and his lady since the days of President Washington. His administration and that of John Adams held ceremonious levees on several occasions. But it was President Thomas Jefferson who began the tradition of the New Year's Day reception. He had abandoned all other levees, "but on the first day of the year, Mr. Jefferson had the doors of the White House thrown open and received all who chose to call upon him."[113] The practice was then continued, and by the time of the Lincoln administration, it had become a time-honored and expected tradition.

Their first New Year's Day reception began at 11 A.M. when the members of the cabinet and their families entered the White House. They were followed by the "gold braided diplomatic corps, justices of the Supreme Court, and officers of the Army and Navy."[114] At noon, the doors were opened to the general public, and for two hours the President and Mrs. Lincoln greeted all who came to visit.

One guest at the reception was Major W. F. M. Arny, who was the United States Indian Agent in New Mexico. He attended the reception wearing buckskins that were elegantly embroidered with beads. Privately, he presented to Mrs. Lincoln a splendid blanket as a New Year's gift. The blanket "was made by a squaw of a Navajo chief, she having been employed upon it for five months. It is of large size, of wool, the figures upon it being of white, red and blue."[115]

A detailed description of Mary's attire worn on this occasion was not given. However, on January 25, 1862, *Harper's Weekly* published a two-page engraving (sketched by Mr. A. Waud) of a White House reception. A latter publication identifies the reception as the New Year's Day Reception.[116] The scene depicts several members of the military in the room as well as members of the Supreme Court.

The artist must have been positioned behind the receiving line when creating this engraving, for the faces of the guests are the focal point. Only the back of Mary's robe is visible. It is shown as a dark-colored robe with a small train gently piled behind her. The skirt panels show deep pleats at the waist. Many dresses made from a heavy material, such as velvet, were often gored at the sides and box-pleated behind.[117] The engraving does not offer such details.

The dress bodice has a back closure; the lacing cord appears in the engraving. The bodice waist is round in the back, not pointed. Most likely the bodice front was pointed. The pagoda sleeves appear to be trimmed with a fabric trim. There is a piece of lace around the neckline of the bodice. However, since the view is only from the back, it is not known if this is a lace collar, a fichu, or a lace trim.

Mary's headdress is a large ribbon fastened in a large bow at the back of the head. The ribbon strings fall well below her shoulders and the crown of the headdress is enhanced with what appears to be leaves and a few flowers.

Lilac Gown
January 7 or 14, 1862

As at all White House functions, journalists from across the country attended these events to report who was there and what was worn, as well as the official events of the evening. One such journalist was Laura Catherine Redden (later Mrs. Searing) who wrote under the pen name Howard Glyndon. During the Civil War Miss Redden was a Washington correspondent for the *St. Louis Republican* newspaper.

Miss Redden attended one grand affair held in the Executive Mansion's Blue Room. During the month of January, receptions were held weekly. While it is not known exactly which event Miss Redden attended, at any of them she would have found Mary dressed most fashionably. During her visit to the White House, Miss Redden described Mrs. Lincoln elaborate lilac dress.

It was made very *décolleté* as to the shoulders, bust, and arms; but she had a certain dimpled chubbiness as to these which justified the style. That portion of her skin visible was of a becoming whiteness. At all events, the charm of her face was not owing to cosmetics. It was a chubby, good-natured face. It was the face of a woman who enjoyed life, a good joke, good eating, fine clothes, and fine horses and carriages, and luxurious surroundings, but it was also the face of a woman whose affectionate nature was predominant. You might safely take your oath that she would be fussy on occasion, but the clouds would not last long with her, and she would soon be laughing as heartily as ever. There is no doubt but that Mr. Lincoln found in her, despite her foibles and sometimes her puerileness, just what he needed, and that she was a most loyal wife and mother and a good woman.[118]

It was not unusual for a newspaper correspondent to focus so much on the character, personality, or even the political loyalties of Mrs. Lincoln.

Pure White Dress
January 21, 1862

The evening of January 21, 1862, the Lincolns held another public reception at the White House. The newspapers reported that the President was in fine spirits that evening.

Mary's costume for the evening was described as "pure white, her dress being an elegant white figured brocade."[119] This may be the same dress Julia Taft referred to when she wrote that Mary was "dressed for that occasion in a beautiful white satin with train and expansive hoops, flowers in her hair, and white gloves."[120]

The month of January was a hectic social time for the Lincolns as events were held on January 7, January 14, January 21, and January 28. These evening levees were in addition to the grand reception held at the Executive Mansion on New Year's Day.

Azure Silk with Velvet Leaves
January 28, 1862

At a levee held in the Blue Room of the Executive Mansion, President Lincoln shook hands for two hours. Dancing followed later that evening. It was customary for the President to lead the promenade with a woman other than his wife — usually the wife of a political ally. This particular evening, Lincoln led the promenade with the wife of Senator Chandler of Michigan.

The press reported that the Red, Blue, Green, and East Rooms of the White House were resplendent and that Mary Lincoln's costume was exquisite. Her gown was described as "azure silk, shot with white, mottled with gorgeous velvet leaves of a deeper blue. A shawl of point lace hung over her arm, and a point lace bertha, of marvelous fibrous texture, encircled her neck. Her ornaments were pearl bracelets and necklace; her head dress of blue and white plumes."[121]

It was said that the President retired early that evening.

Evening Gown with Lace Bertha
1861 or 1862

An engraved portrait of Mrs. Lincoln wearing an evening costume was published in November of 1862. The paper stated, "We publish herewith a portrait of Mrs. Lincoln, wife of the President of the United States, from a photograph by Brady."[122] Unfortunately, the original photograph is currently missing.

As her son Willie had died nine months earlier, Mary was in full mourning and did not attend social functions at the time of this publication. The newspaper used an earlier photograph for their image, but they did not say when the photograph was taken. No mention of the dress style or color was included.

The dress is similar in style to the one worn at the grand ball in February, but there are some differences in design. The evening gown in the engraving has a fashionably low neckline trimmed with two slightly gathered rows of lace, each about six inches deep. The bodice has a center back closure, and the bodice front is a smooth silk. The fashionable long point is at the waist of the center front. Mary wears a floral bouquet at the center front of the neckline.

The back panels of the skirt include a long silk train at least one yard in length. The skirt's trimming consists of one eighteen-inch-deep lace flounce and bows. The top of the flounce is placed at finger-tip length on the skirt and encircles the skirt, whereas the ball gown worn on February 5 had a flounce artistically draped between the skirt panels.

The engraving shows four large silk bows at the top edge of the lace flounce, which most likely had three others not visible to view. They seem to be placed on the seam lines of the gored skirt. Engravers sometimes changed or left out small details of a photograph they worked from to make a more pleasing product, not appreciating that future historians would need their work for documentation. Either way, Mary's dress style was keeping with the fashion magazines of the day which encouraged ball gowns to be "profusely trimmed with lace and flowers."[123]

Evening Gown with Lace Bertha, 1861 or 1862. (*Harper's Weekly* engraving, November 1862, author's collection)

Mary's evening costume also includes a diadem of flowers, pearl jewelry, and a white handkerchief.

White Silk with Black Lace
February 5, 1862

Due to the thousands of people who had moved into Washington for military operations and the war effort, the city was overflowing. The public receptions of the past where anyone could come and meet the President were now suffering from want of crowd control. It was not unusual for three thousand or more people to attend any White House public reception and wish to shake hands with the President. Lincoln often complained that his hand was swollen from shaking hands with so many visitors. There was also the expense of the receptions to consider. Every reception guest expected to receive more than a mere cup of tea and a cookie. Newspapers criticized Mrs. Lincoln for entertaining due to war expenses. Funds would be better spent feeding the soldiers than politicians. However, newspapers also criticized her for not entertaining because receptions boosted public morale. Public receptions were also traditional; and traditions were difficult to break in Washington. This tradition was started, according to one reporter, out of "a false deference to the false notion of democratic equality which certainly is practiced by no private family, however humble, and which no one has a right to exact from that of the President."[124] However, it was a time of war, and one had to consider the President's safety as well. Perhaps, for the sake of the President's life and for the well-being of his hands, it was time for a change.

Receptions were held almost weekly during the winter months. Mrs. Lincoln decided to change tradition and have a party instead of a public reception. Lincoln was coming into the second year of his presidency. Mary's carefully planned renovations to the White House were completed after months of work, and it was time to celebrate. In January 1862, invitations were issued to between six hundred and seven hundred people to attend a ball to be held on Wednesday, February 5.[125]

Early that evening, guests began to form a long line of carriages to the White House. As the guests arrived, they were greeted by doormen who were wearing solferino-colored coats that matched the trim on the new White House china. Guests were then "passed to the second story of the mansion, which had been thrown open for dressing rooms. Thence they returned to the grand entrance, and were shown into the Blue Room, whence they passed to the grand saloon, or East Room, where they were received by Mr. and Mrs. Lincoln with a gracious welcome and a kind word."[126]

Mary's dress was described as a "lustrous white satin dress with a train a yard in length, trimmed with one deep flounce of the richest black Chantilly lace. The dress was, of course, décolleté with short sleeves, displaying the exquisitely molded shoulders of our fair 'Republican Queen.' "[127]

The gown's bodice had a long point at the waist of the center front. The short sleeves were trimmed with two rows of black lace. One row was located at the seam line; the other located at the lower edge of the sleeve. The neckline of the bodice was finished with the same narrow trim that graced the top of the skirt's lace flounce. A silk bow adorned the top of each sleeve.

The black Chantilly lace on the gored skirt was approximately eighteen inches deep. It was looped up six times with black and white bows. From newspaper engravings it appears bows alternated in color as they circled the skirt — three being white and three being black. The top edge of the black lace flounce is finished with a narrow trim.

Mary wore a bouquet of crêpe myrtle at the center front of her bodice and had a bunch of crêpe myrtle on the right side of her skirt. From the left side of the waist hung what may have been a sash or a girdle pocket. These could be used to carry a handkerchief and portmonnaie. Mary's is made from white silk and trimmed with the same black lace that trims her bodice.

White Silk with Black Lace, February 5, 1862. (Engraving from *Leslie's*, February 22, 1862, author's collection)

Her diadem consisted of black and white flowers. Following the etiquette required for holding a fan, Mary's feather fan is held in her left hand indicating she was a married woman. Her costume was complete with a necklace, earrings, brooch, and bracelets made of pearl.

Mrs. Keckley helped Mary dress for the ball that evening. While Mary was finishing her preparations, Mr. Lincoln patiently waited for her. Standing by the fireplace with hands clasped behind his back, he stared at the carpet. When Mary began to walk, "the rustling of the satin dress attracted his attention. He looked at it a few moments; then in his quaint, quite way remarked, 'Whew! Our cat has a long tail tonight. Mother, it is my opinion, if some of that tail was nearer the head, it would be in better style.' "128

For once, most of the newspapers were much kinder to Mrs. Lincoln than they usually were. The idea of Madame President 'giving' a ball for selected guests had been untried in the social customs of Washington. Mary's idea was considered "a very respectful if not a brilliant success." *The Washington Star* reporter felt it was the "most superb affair of its kind ever seen here."129

The praise for the event was well deserved, but it was also hollow for the family. For while the Marine Band played "Mary Lincoln's Polka," a tune they composed just for the occasion, and the guests enjoyed a midnight supper, Willie Lincoln lay in his bed very ill. Within a few days, the shadow of death would claim the life of eleven-year-old Willie, and the White House family would be plunged into the deepest despair. Mary, the grieving mother, tossed aside all elaborate parties, entertainments, and social events. Her fashionable costumes were cast aside for mourning attire, and for nearly two years Mary wore black.

Mourning Customs in General

The theological revolution commonly known as "The Great Awakening" taught that death was a joyous occasion to be celebrated. It was the promised salvation and reunion with family members who had previously passed through the thin veil that separated the living and the lost. Many ministers preached that Heaven was a "place in which families were reunited, homes restored, and nurseries existed to care for children who died before their parents."[130] Death was celebrated as a tribute to life, and the Victorians openly accepted it, making it a "part of daily living through mourning practices."[131]

The nineteenth-century woman's sphere included the home, family, religion, morality, and respectability. Death was a religious issue. Therefore, following acceptable mourning customs fell into the woman's sphere.

A lack of medical knowledge, childhood diseases, and a high mortality rate among women of childbearing age, were all factors in a high mortality rate. Most deaths and visitations occurred in the home. The Civil War claimed more than six hundred thousand lives and every family knew someone killed in battle. Mourning rituals were expected to be followed for each family member. For the Victorian woman, mourning was more than a ritual, it was often a way of life.

Black had long been the traditional color of mourning. Women donned elaborate black apparel and were expected to follow fashion "according to what they could afford, and the expectations of their family and community."[132] A widower may wear a black suit for three months. A black suit was also normal business attire, so most often a man wore a black mourning band around his arm or his hat. Children were also expected to participate in mourning customs in the same manner as adults. Young children under the age of twelve wore white in the summer and gray in the winter. Their clothing was trimmed with black buttons, ruffles, belts, and bonnet ribbons. Even an infant's white clothing was trimmed with black embroidery or ribbon to indicate mourning.[133] It was thought that "grieving for the dead in clothing designed especially

76

for mourning linked the family together and set them apart from secular society."[134]

A woman observed four stages of mourning, each with its own fashion, customs, and rules of etiquette for social behavior. During all stages of mourning a lady was expected to wear the most current fashions. The length of time observed in each stage was determined by a woman's relationship to the deceased. Not all women in black were widows. Mourning was also worn for parents, siblings, children, in-laws, grandparents, aunts, uncles, cousins, and even the parents of a husband's first wife.

A woman in her first stage of mourning for her husband was expected to cancel all social engagements within twenty-four hours. A widow dressed in black from her head to her toe. While undergarments were white, some women trimmed them with black ribbon or embroidery to show that a woman's grief had penetrated to the innermost sanctuaries. Acceptable mourning fabrics were bombazine, paramatta, Henrietta cloth, wool, and dull cotton, for they lacked any type of sheen. The most suitable color during this first stage of mourning was "dead black." Another suitable fashion was for a widow's dress to be "covered with crape as a part of its construction."[135] Crape was also used for cuffs, collars, and other dress trim.

Accessories such as gloves, muffs, shawls, and reticules were also black. One of the most important parts of a lady's mourning costume was her bonnet and veil. The veil fell from the crown of the bonnet to the shoulder, elbow, waist, or even mid-calf depending on the woman's preference.[136] If a lady could not avoid going out in public, or when she was en route to church, the veil was worn over her face. This was a request for privacy and indicated that others should not speak to her, or to speak only in hushed tones.

Widows were expected to wear deepest mourning for at least a year. A mother who lost a child wore the darkest crape for six months. Slowly, a woman came out of her mourning. First she was allowed to wear shiny materials such as black silk and add black trims and mourning jewelry to her costume. Mourning jewelry was mass-produced with "symbolisms such as wreaths, leaves, shamrocks, crosses, anchors" and other symbols indicating mourning.[137] A cut rose indicated a life cut short; a sheaf of wheat signified a long life. Also popular were weeping willow trees, clasped hands, knots, and ivy. Hair jewelry was often made using the hair of the deceased.

In her final stages of mourning, a lady added deep violet or purple and grey to her wardrobe, followed by white trims. Over the next few months, she could add white, stone-gray, and lavender to her costumes. Shiny jewelry made from gold, pearls, amethyst, and hair was worn during this final stage.

A widow was expected to wear mourning attire for about two and a half years. A mother was in mourning for at least a year, while a woman mourned her siblings for about six months. Often, just as a woman was entering her final stage of mourning for one relative, another one would pass away and the ritual began again, thus placing the woman in a perpetual state of mourning.

Mary's Mourning

Willie Lincoln died at five in the afternoon on February 20, 1862, from bilious fever, which was probably either typhoid or acute malarial infection. While both parents were thrown in to a deep depression and grief over the lost of the boy, it was Mary's wailing for Willie that could be heard throughout the White House walls. The boy's body lay in state in the Green Room. His funeral, the first White House funeral for a child, was held in the East Room — the same room where just days before Mary and others had danced. Mary remained in seclusion for days, unable to even gather the strength to attend her son's funeral.[138]

Robert sent word to his Aunt Elizabeth Edwards to come to help care for Mary. The day of the funeral, Elizabeth boarded a train in Springfield and headed east for Washington. The eldest of the family,

Elizabeth had been like a mother to Mary after the death of their own mother. Robert believed if anyone could help Mary through this difficult period of grief, it was she.

By February 28, Elizabeth had arrived in Washington where she found Mary "utterly unable to control her feelings."[139] Mary had confined herself to her room and her own bed. She was so distraught that she was unable to take care of Tad who was suffering from the same illness that had taken Willie. By March 2, Tad was feeling better, but was still ill. Elizabeth knew that her presence was soothing to Mary. In a letter to her daughter, Elizabeth explained how a little more than a week after Willie's death, she had compassionately, "persuaded her (Mary) to put on the black dress, that so freshly and painfully reminded of the loss, that will long shadow her pleasures. Such is her nature, that I can not realize that she will forgo them all, or even long, under existing circumstances."[140]

Elizabeth was wrong, for Mary would remain in mourning beyond the expectations of society. All receptions were cancelled for the remaining of the year as were the band concerts held on the White House lawn. The public could not be pleased. People who had earlier criticized Mary for holding public receptions during war time now complained about the lack of entertainment. A compromise was reached and the Marine Band performed in Lafayette Square across from the White House.[141]

With her sister by her side, Mary slowly regained her composure. By March 20, newspapers reported that Mrs. Lincoln had been confined to her room since her son's death but now was "almost back to normal health" and by March 21, she was receiving nonrelated visitors.[142] Having relatives cheered Mary and helped her regain health and strength, and after Willie's death she was blessed with having an abundance of family surround her. One observer noted the White House had guests and Mrs. Lincoln was surrounded by "a dozen Todds of the Edwards breed."[143] By the end of Elizabeth's visit, Mary had been sight-seeing with family members to Mount Vernon, had sent floral bouquets to friends, and had accompanied the President on a routine carriage ride to the Navy Yard.

Elizabeth and her Edwards entourage had accomplished their mission and left Mary still a grieving mother but better able to handle her situation.

During the summer months, the Lincoln family moved into the Anderson Cottage at the Soldiers' Home. There they were just a short carriage ride away from the dirt, disease and din of the city, but still far enough away to leave some of their problems in Washington. When Laura Redden visited, Mary was wearing "deep black." Mary was still in her first stage of mourning.[144]

It is unclear exactly how long Mary remained in mourning attire for Willie. Some historians believe that she emerged from her mourning around 1864, or even as late as 1865. Others believe that she remained in mourning and only put aside her mourning attire for special occasions such as the wedding reception for General Tom Thumb and Lavinia Warren. In 1864, Walt Whitman often saw the Lincolns as they rode from the Soldiers' Home to the city. He commented that Mary was "in complete black with a long crape veil"[145] typical of mourning attire. Mary did exceed the one year required mourning a mother displayed for her child. She also became a victim of perpetual mourning. Two of her half-brothers and a brother-in-law were killed during battle during the course of the war. Samuel, the first killed in battle, died in April 1862, just under two months after Willie's death. By the end of the summer, Mary's youngest half-brother, Alexander, had also died. It is doubtful Mary would have donned mourning attire for any of these relatives as they were all Confederate soldiers. Even if she mourned for them in her heart, the public would have been endlessly critical if she had mourned them in public. However, she did have other relatives who died during this time. Her closest relative was her older brother Levi, a Union supporter who died in October 1864, and it is probable Mary donned mourning attire in memory of him. It is also likely that Mary was mourning her brother when Walt Whitman wrote of her attire.

Black Velvet
January 1, 1863

The lady of the White House may have been in mourning, but the public clamored for the public receptions to be reinstated. Plans were made, and the annual New Year's Day reception would be the first public reception held since Willie's death. Thousands of people attended. President Lincoln signed his Emancipation Proclamation this day.

The newspapers were filled with stories about the Emancipation Proclamation, and for once, Mary's attire was not mentioned. Prior to the event, Mrs. John A. Kasson had announced in the *Iowa State Register* that "the President's Lady would receive calls at the White House on January 1 in black velvet, trimmed with thread lace."[146]

Mr. Benjamin French, the Commissioner of Public Buildings, stood beside Mary during the reception and presented visitors to her. He later wrote that Mary turned to him and sadly said, "Oh, Mr. French, how much we have passed through since last we stood here."[147] And indeed, Mary had endured much during the past year. Not only had she lost her beloved Willie, but also her two half-brothers killed while fighting for the Confederate forces. Newspaper reporters and Washington gossips were quick to label Mary a Confederate sympathizer because of the actions of her brothers. The emotions of the day overwhelmed her. Mr. French reported that Mary "seemed much affected through the first part of the reception and was too much overcome by her feelings to remain until it ended."[148]

Pink Silk
February 13, 1863

Charles Sherwood Stratton was the diminutive protégé of circus pioneer P. T. Barnum. Using the moniker General Tom Thumb, Stratton dressed like historical characters, sang, danced, and entertained audiences in both the United States and in England. His engagement to fellow performer Lavinia Warren captured the attention of the general public. Barnum, forever the promoter, placed articles in the New York newspapers about the upcoming nuptials on February 10, 1863, including engravings of many of the bridal gifts the couple received. Two thousand wedding guests crowed into the New York church to witness the ceremony. It was Barnum's intent to have the couple presented to the leaders of several nations, since the publicity was wonderful for his circus.

During the couple's honeymoon trip they traveled to Washington City and stayed at the Willard Hotel. Mary was convinced by her advisors that is was her duty to entertain the famous couple. She therefore scheduled a reception to be held in the East Room on February 13, 1863. One attendee later wrote to his sister-in-law, "Mrs. Lincoln, excellent lady that she is, sent & invited us all up . . . to see Tom & his bride." This was considered a small affair; about fifty guests were in attendance.[149]

Mary may have felt that it was her duty to entertain the famous couple, but her son, Robert, felt differently. When asked if he would attend the reception, he replied, "No, Mother. I do not propose to assist in entertaining Tom Thumb. My notions of duty, perhaps, are somewhat different from yours."[150]

Tad, who did attend the reception, could not help but notice the similarities between Mrs. Lincoln and Mrs. Stratton. As the Lincolns sat on the sofa with their honored guests, Tad commented, "Mother, if you were a little woman like Mrs. Stratton you would look just like her."

Another guest commented about Mary's appearance by saying, "Mary Lincoln's black mourning clothes for Willie are finally gone."

Mary attended the reception wearing a low-necked, pink silk gown.[151] Another source described Mary's costume as "rose-colored, low-necked frock, with hoops, and wearing pink flowers in her hair."[152] To the eyes of many men, there is little difference between pink and rose.

The next day, Mary again would wear black.

Bonnet
March 27, 1863

President Lincoln met with a group of Indian chiefs in the East Room on March 27, 1863. That same day, the chiefs posed for a photograph with several representatives of Washington society in the White House conservatory. The woman on the far right with the sunlight shining on her face is Mary Lincoln.

Her entire costume is not visible due to her placement in the back row. A glimpse of a white collar is visible and the fabric of a dark colored garment. What is visible is her bonnet. Beginning in 1862, fashion advisors recommended that a bonnet be heavily trimmed with flowers, to "resemble a garden in full bloom."[153] Even though Mary was still mourning Willie at the time this photograph was taken, her bonnet is fashionably trimmed with flowers. A spray of white flowers is visible on the left side of Mary's hair, and some small darker flowers are on the right. According to mourning customs of the time, a cluster of white flowers indicated mourning for a child.

Mary's bonnet strings are a dark color (probably black) with white trim. What is most significant about the bonnet strings is that they are the same ones Mary wears in the photograph identified as ML, O-25. Since Mary wore the same bonnet strings in both photographs, they would have been taken during the same season.

Bonnet, March, 27, 1862. (Photograph courtesy of The Lincoln Museum, Fort Wayne, IN. (Reference #4605) [identified as ML, O-22])

Black Dress with Bonnet and Veil
Circa 1862 or 1863

General standards for mourning included clothing with little or no ornament. In this photograph, Mary is wearing mourning attire softened with white accents which were used when mourning children. White symbolized the deceased child's purity and innocence.

Mary's bonnet includes black silk flowers and white flowers. The veil when pulled over Mary's face would provide protection from dust and dirt as well as privacy from onlookers. Her bonnet strings are black edged with white.

The day dress bodice is typical of the fashions popular in 1862 and 1863. It is high and plain with a front closure. About twelve shiny, plain, buttons are sewn on the right side of the closure. The buttons are ornamental as the bodice closes with hooks and eyes. With rich, expensive fabrics, expansive pagoda sleeves were most fashionable. These used more fabric than closed sleeves and indicated the wealth or social status of the wearer. Mary wears white undersleeves under her pagoda sleeves. Her small white collar is closed with a black brooch.

The folds in the fabric indicate pleating at the waistline of the skirt. There are no trims or embellishments on the skirt. During this era, it was fashionable to trim a skirt with a Greek pattern or a deep line of quilling above the hem. These decorative trims were often a contrasting color from the fashion fabric.[154] Since Mary was mourning Willie, any type of fancy trim would have been inappropriate.

Black Dress with Bonnet and Veil, Circa 1862 or 1863. (Photograph courtesy of The Lincoln Museum, Fort Wayne, Indiana (Reference #100) [identified as ML, O-25])

Day Dress
Circa 1862 or 1863

This particular carte de visite is simply marked "Mrs. Lincoln" at the bottom. However, William H. Mumler, a photographer from Boston, used this same photo to print cartes de visite on card stock dated 1865. Again, it appears that a previous photo was used on newer card stock thus making determining a date for the sitting difficult. Some historians believe this photograph was taken in 1861.[155] A close look at Mary's clothing and hairstyle reveal fashions which more closely resemble the styles of 1862 and 1863. Close examination also reveals that Mary is wearing the same dress bodice as she is in photograph ML, O-25.

As Mary remained in mourning for her son Willie for well over the socially required year of mourning, if this photograph was taken in 1862 or 1863, the dress would have been black.

The bodice is a plain high bodice. It has what appears to be a hook-and-eye front closure with a row of small, plain buttons down the center front. The buttons are decorative and not functional. Her collar is a narrow white collar most likely made of linen. It is fastened with a small black brooch that has a white dot. This may have been a pearl, for pearls were considered appropriate for mourning jewelry and represented tears.

Mary's hair style, though far from extravagant, is typical of those from 1862 and 1863. Her hair has a center part and is pulled up in side puffs with an invisible net.[156] A lace snood or other hair covering is visible at the back of her head. It was unladylike for a woman's ears to show and Mary's are appropriately covered.

In 1862 and 1863, as the war raged on, day attire became more plain and simple. One fashion advisor suggested, "The morning dress is more than ever simple and in the street a lady ought to appear, as it were, incognito."[157] In this photo, Mary follows this guideline explicitly, and could easily be mistaken for a common housewife. She is not dressed for a ball or social event. She is not posing for a photograph as the

Day Dress, Circa 1862 or 1863. (Photo courtesy of the Edward Norton Collection [identified as ML, O-7])

President's wife. She is simply a wife and mother, and possibly a mother in mourning, just like so many other women in the country.

Riding Habit
August 6, 1863

The Washington heat was stifling in the summer of 1863. Heat, thousands of soldiers and horses, poor sewage drainage, and the swelled population from the war effort, made Washington hot, dirty, smelly, and unbearable. Mary, who had just recovered from a carriage accident, Robert, and Tad traveled north for relief from the city. They stayed at the Tip Top Hotel in the White Mountains of New Hampshire. This area had become a popular tourist attraction during the 1850s. Special coaches carried people on sightseeing adventures. Mary traveled in a group of a hundred and thirty visitors who had come to enjoy the cooler temperatures and sights of nature including the Flume, the Old Man of the Rock, mountains, and valleys.

A newspaper article tells the story of Mrs. Lincoln coming up to the desk and asking for a piece of paper to write a letter home to her husband. She also requested a piece of rock to carry. When the desk clerk offered to send the rock with her driver, Mary cheerfully replied, "No, every lady should have a great pocket." For ten minutes, Mary carefully chose her words to compose her letter. When handing the pen back to the desk clerk, she added, "I am sorry to trouble you, but you know a woman's letter is incomplete without a postscript."[158]

"She was dressed in a dark chequered [sic] riding habit, dark bonnet and veil. She has a very fair cheerful smiling face, which does one good to look upon. She is quite light complexioned, has blue eyes and dark auburn hair, and on the whole, as might be hoped and expected of a President's wife, has a pleasant agreeable way."[159]

Riding habits were made from a sturdy, easy-to-clean fabric. Black and dark blue were popular colors. Fashion advisors suggested a "corsage without basques, sleeves wide at the ends; cambric collar and turned back cuffs."[160] The skirt might be a few inches shorter than a day dress, but not so short as to reveal too much of the boot-clad leg.

An 1863 *Godey's* fashion plate depicts a riding habit made from black cloth. The sleeve cuffs are turned back and trimmed with fluted worsted braid and large gilt buttons. Large lapels are also trimmed with the same braid as is the bottom edge of the basque. Three large buttons close the front. The waist is quite short and square in front, revealing a belt and the bottom half of the cashmere vest. Ruching edges the bottom of the vest. A white blouse or chemisette is visible beneath the bodice's lapels, and a scarlet ribbon is tied around the neck. Undersleeves and thick gloves are worn. A reticule, to hold a lady's essentials, hangs from the belt.[161] A rider usually wore a dark hat to complete her outfit, often with a veil to help shield a lady's face from the dust and dirt of the road.

Emily's Letter
December 13 – 14, 1863

When Confederate Brigadier General Benjamin Hardin Helm was killed in battle at Chickamauga in September 1863, it was told that President Lincoln wept and said, "I feel as David of old did when he was told of the death of Absalom."[162] Helm was the husband to Mary's younger half-sister, Emily whom Lincoln had affectionately dubbed "Little Sister." When Emily had visited her sisters in Springfield less than a decade earlier, Abraham and Mary had treated her like a daughter. Now, Little Sister was a widow with three small children.

Prior to her husband's death, Emily had traveled throughout the South helping the troops in whatever way she could. At the time of Ben's death, Emily was visiting her sisters who lived in Selma, Alabama. She was summoned to Atlanta, Georgia for her husband's funeral. Afterwards, her travel plans were to return with her children to her mother's home in Kentucky. In route, she was stopped at Fortress Monroe, Virginia, where she was told she would have to take an oath of allegiance to the United States government in order to continue further. She refused. A telegram was sent to the White House asking the President what to do. He replied with a short telegram which stated simply, but authoritatively, "Send her to me, A. LINCOLN."

When Emily and her six-year-old daughter Katherine arrived in Washington, they were greeted warmly by Abraham and Mary. Emily was donned in the heavy mourning crape of a widow.

Emily kept a diary during her visit to the White House and throughout the Civil War. Years later, when her daughter Katherine wrote her biography, *Mary, Wife of Lincoln*, Emily gave her access to notes from the diary. When the book was completed, Emily burned the original diary for it contained too much bitterness and she did not want others to read it. Katherine used the notes to weave together the stories from Emily's short visit to Washington. Her book tells a readable tale, but the notes that remained unused gave vivid details — especially about Mary's wardrobe.

Emily noted that on the evening of December 13, General Sickles came to call. Mary was receiving guests in the Red Room which was used as a drawing room. The furnishing included "a grand piano and Washington's portrait which Mrs. Madison cut out to save from the British is in this room — everything is crimson."[163]

On this evening, Mary wore a black and white gown with a shot silk point lace collar. Trimming around the skirt consisted of stripes of black velvet and buttons made of a "light white made with a shade of black." Emily's description of the buttons is vague. Perhaps she meant they were white buttons with black around the edges. The dress was to be worn at intimate White House dinners. Mary also wore a bonnet trimmed with "black and white flowers, and a mantle — a quilted cloak."[164]

The next day (December 14) Mary showed Emily the dresses that would be worn at White House functions during the party season. Emily wrote:

> This morning she showed me all her handsome dresses. She will wear purple this winter, and has a magnificent purple velvet to make up for New Years. She has a beautiful purple silk and purple morning costume — low and high necks. Beautifully trimmed skirts are very much trimmed. Her laces are beautiful. A shawl of white costs 2,500, and elegant black one, lace veils and beautiful sets (one particularly of La Pensée handkerchiefs & all very pretty hankies) . . . bonnets of purple velvet, of white and purple, and head dresses of every variety. The purple being the great color.[165]

It is unclear whether Mary wore purple because she was wearing half-mourning, or if she preferred purple as a fashionable color. She did choose to wear a royal purple dress at three of her four New Year's Day receptions. The only time she wore a different color at this event was when she was wearing black and mourning her son.

The last diary entry written during Emily's stay was dated December 14. After staying with the Lincoln's for about a week, Emily was ready to return to Kentucky, her other two children, and her mother. Lincoln gave her a pass to complete her journey. This pass restored Emily's rights and protected her as a loyal citizen. The small framed widow, dressed in heavy crape, bonnet, and veil, bid a sad farewell to the Lincolns. Little Sister and Mary never saw one another again.

Black Silk
December 29, 1863

A few days after Christmas, a brief news article reported "Mrs. Lincoln was at the Capitol on Tuesday morning, dressed in a black silk dress with sweeping skirts and handsome furs. Senator Sumner and other Congressional gentlemen paid their respects to her in the marble room of the north extension."[166] The type of furs Mary wore is not mentioned. Popular winter furs, especially for muffs, were sable and ermine[167].

A *Godey's* fashion plate for the winter of 1863 depicts a sacque and petticoat style, outdoor costume with fur trim. The trim is placed at the sleeve cuffs, around the neckline, down the front closure of the bodice, and around the bodice hem. Other types of fashionable furs were long boas and muffs. Whether or not Mary owned a costume such as the one featured in *Godey's* is not known. From the old clothes sale, it is known that Mary owned a Russian sable boa, a Russian sable cape, and a set of furs consisting of a sable cape, cuffs, and muff.[168] These were not the only furs in Mrs. Lincoln's wardrobe; she also owned several garments made from ermine and garments made of unidentified fur.

Purple Trimmed with Black Velvet
January 1, 1864

Special preparations were made for the New Year's Day reception. The newspapers reported that linen coverings were placed over the carpets to protect them from the thousands of feet that would trod upon them, probably with slush and mud on the soles. Decorations were placed, and two large American flags were draped over the front entrance of the White House. One of the more elaborate preparations was to provide a temporary exit door to the East Room. The sashes were removed from a large window, and a bridge was placed across the area which allowed people to leave successfully and safely through the window.[169] Extraordinary crowd sizes often caused the parlors and halls of the White House to be jammed with people.

As guests entered the White House, they were moved to the Blue Room. They were presented to Mr. Lincoln, and then to Mrs. Lincoln. It was noted that Mary wore "a purple dress trimmed with black velvet and lace, with an exquisite lace neck-tie, fastened with a pearl brooch — her head-dress was ornamented with a white plume."[170] Since this dress has a neck-tie, it was a day dress. The special laces and trimmings made it fashionable and appropriate to wear as a visiting dress.

In his descriptions of the New Year's Day reception, Noah Brooks gave a slightly different description of Mary's dress. His column in the February 4, 1864, issue of the Sacramento *Daily Union*, Mr. Brooks appealed to his female readers by writing:

> My feminine readers will be interested to know that Mrs. Lincoln wore a purple velvet dress, decorated with white satin fluting (isn't that what you call it?) around the bottom; Valenciennes lace was on the sleeves, and an immense train flowed out behind. Mrs. Lincoln never looked better than in the dark rich tones of her reception dress, in which she has, for the first time, left off her mourning garb. . . .[171]

At first, it may appear that these descriptions are for two separate dresses. However, each newspaper correspondent describes the New Year's Day reception in the same manner. The differences then are simply the result of two people looking at the same item and each seeing details the other does not. Lace trim is mentioned in both descriptions. Mr. Brooks informed his readers that there was lace trim on the lower portion of the skirt. He is also unsure if this trim is correctly called "flutings" which explains why this is not mentioned in the *Chicago Tribune*. Mr. Brooks does not mention Mary's headdress, but another guest noted it was "ornamented with a white plume" matching the description given in the *Tribune*.[172]

The fabric choice is unclear. Mary had shown Emily a purple velvet dress that she planned to wear on New Year's Day. One reporter states it is a purple dress trimmed with black velvet while the other states it is a purple velvet dress. Both reporters could be accurate. The dress may have been purple velvet trimmed with black velvet. Another possibility is that one of the accounts is incorrect in regards to the fabric choice. The people who wrote about fashion in period newspapers were seldom the most well-qualified to do so.

No matter which fabric description is correct, Noah Brooks was probably correct when he stated that Mary had never looked better than she did in this gown. However, he was incorrect to say that it was the first time Mary had not worn mourning attire since Willie had died. She had put her mourning aside for various occasions and events prior to this reception, though this may have been the official end to her mourning wardrobe for daywear as well as special occasions.

Dark Dress with Jeweled Headdress Circa 1864

Little is known of this photograph. In his 1968 publication, Lloyd Ostendorf gave supporting research indicating this photograph was most likely taken in 1864 by the Washington, D.C., firm of Wenderoth and Taylor. Years later, he identified the photograph as having been taken by "an unknown artist, Springfield, about 1860," but offered no explanation as to the change in the date.[173]

Mary's hairstyle is this photograph became popular in 1863 when coiffures became more elaborate than in previous years, and curls were worn at the back of the head. For women who did not have hair long

Dark Dress with Jeweled Headdress, Circa 1864. (Photograph courtesy of The Lincoln Museum, Fort Wayne, Indiana (Reference #4598). [Photo identified as ML, O-24]

enough to wear curls, or for those who just wanted to add more fullness to their existing hair, false curls were purchased. By 1864, fashions magazines advised women, "False curls, plaits and bows, and false masses at the back are as necessary as the crinoline."[174]

The jeweled headdress Mary wears is the same one she wore in photograph ML, O-4. The headdress consists of seven large dark colored stones encircled by seed pearls. From each large jewel hangs a smaller matching jewel. A metal band circles the head and connects together at the back of the head with a large fabric bow. Another larger jewel is placed on the metal band near the ear lob. Another band runs across the head indicating that this style of headdress was worn with the hair in a bun or knot that sat low on the back of the head.

Mary's large dangling earrings match the jewels of the headdress. They reflect the fashion of 1864 when larger earrings came into vogue. A strand of pearls is worn with her costume. It appears that her brooch may be attached to the pearls. It was common for a lady's necklace to include a removable brooch which could be worn with or without the necklace.

Little can be determined about Mary's day dress. It is a dark color, and since Mary wore this parure set with other black dresses, this robe may have been black as well. The bodice has a front hook-and-eye closure. The ornamental buttons have dark centers and are surrounded by what appears to be seed pearls, thus matching the parure set. Mary's white lace collar has a scalloped edge.

Day Dress with Ruching 1864

This engraving by Samuel Sartain, one of the brothers in the famous family of artists, was first published in 1864. Both a full-sized sixteen-by-

Day Dress with Ruching, 1864. (CDV photograph, author's collection.)

eleven-inch engraving and a carte de visite photo of the engraving were sold by the artist. An original photograph for this image has not been found; it was a common practice to destroy the original photographs once an engraving was completed.

In this image, Mary wears a high plain bodice with a front hook-and-eye closure. As many as twelve buttons decorate the front closure, but only ten are visible because Mary's hands rest in her lap, covering the lower edge of the bodice. Two darts on each side of the closure fit the bodice close to the body.

The seam line of the dropped shoulder line is covered with ruching. Her full pagoda sleeves are trimmed with ruching at the cuff. Mary's delicate collar appears to be made of lace with a fine scalloped edge. The plain white undersleeves have a cuff that fits tight at the wrist. Only one small section of the skirt is visible. It appears to fit into the waistband with box pleating.

Mary wears the same parure, consisting of headdress, drop earrings, necklace and brooch, as she wears in photograph ML, O-24. Her hair is parted in the middle and has long curls cascading down her back. Since false curls were popular at the time, it is impossible to know if Mary's curls were her own hair, or were pinned in her coiffure with a comb.

Black and White Taffeta Circa 1863 or 1864

Underneath the alterations made to this dress is an excellent example of a mid-1860s day dress. The provenance of this dress is highly questionable, but it is attributed to Mary Lincoln. The white trim is not original to the dress and the structure of the garment has been altered.

It is believed this was a mourning dress made from black silk taffeta with a woven white crossbar. The window-pane design creates about a three-inch square. The combination of black softened with white could

Black and White Taffeta, Circa 1863 or 1864. (Photo courtesy of Chicago History Museum)

represent mourning for a child, or half-mourning for another relative.

The high bodice is plain with a front closure. Eight small, round white buttons are sewn on to the closure. The sleeves are tight and narrow and closed at the wrist. A small point over the wrist adds interest to a garment that is otherwise very simple. Black lace is located at the sleeve cuff, but it is not certain the lace is original to the dress. A detachable collar is made of black silk and trimmed with white.

The skirt is shown with the waist band worn over the bodice edge, but Mary would have worn the bodice over the waistband. The skirt is elliptical in shape which was fashionable in the mid-1860s. Both the bodice and the skirt are lined with brown cotton. The skirt has a hem facing made of polished cotton. (Location: Chicago History Museum, Chicago, Illinois.)

Black Velvet with Square Neckline Circa 1863 or 1864

On October 3, 1863, President Lincoln declared by proclamation that the last Thursday of November would be set apart and observed "as a day of Thanksgiving and Praise to our beneficent Father who dwelleth in the Heavens."[175] For the next several years, the idea of families setting aside a day for Thanksgiving prompted artists to create images of serene family gatherings, often reading together or engaged in family conversation.

For the Lincoln family, such a portrait never existed in reality. Robert was away at school and later with the military. Willie died before the first year of the Lincoln administration was completed. Still, the public wanted portraits of the Lincoln family depicting them as a complete, happy, intact family. After Lincoln's death, portrait artists rushed to create images of a happy Lincoln family that could be sold to the public. One such portrait was painted by Samuel Bell Waugh. Although original photos are unknown, it is believed this family portrait was painted from photographs that may have been taken in late 1863. In 1866, Waugh's work served as the inspiration for a print produced by William Sartain. The print was then republished as cartes de visite. Sartain's craftsmanship was so life-like that owners of the print often believed they had a true photograph of the Lincolns.[176]

In this portrait Mary is seated in a green upholstered chair on the right side of the table. She wears what appears to be a black velvet dress. Her plain high bodice has a square neckline which is trimmed with either a black lace or black ruching. The bodice has a front closure and appears to have buttons down the center front.

The full sleeves are decorated at the wrist with the same black trim that is placed at the neckline. Mary wears billowing white undersleeves and holds a white handkerchief. Her pleated skirt folds gently in her chair.

Her costume is completed with a delicate necklace and a headdress with a bow that sits at the nap of her neck. Her coiffure is parted in the middle and has long curls on the side and in the back. This same hairstyle was worn by Mary in photograph ML, O-24 and was quite popular during the winter of 1863–1864.

Fashion advisors at this time described the plain high bodice cut square in the front as in vogue. Often a bodice was worn with a jacket. Skirts were set "in full gathers at the back and small pleats at the sides." The most fashionable skirts often had a hem edge as large as 6 yards (216 inches) in circumference.[177] Since fabric was often 25 inches in width, a fashionable skirt could have as many as 9 panels, using 11 or more yards of fabric, to reach this enormous circumference.

Such excess showed that affluent members of society could afford luxuries such as expensive fabrics made into massive skirts. In addition, a person wearing such an outfit could not be expected to do any sort of manual labor, but would depend on hired servants to run the household and care for the family's needs. Members of the aristocracy dressed as well as their purses would allow. Mary Lincoln was no exception.

Black Silk with Trim
Circa 1864

Past historians identify this photograph of Mary Lincoln has having been taken in 1863 in Washington. The stereograph card of this image, which was published by E. & H. T. Anthony Company, is dated 1865.[178] While it is possible this image was taken in 1863 and the cards later printed by the photographer, the style of the dress design more closely resembles the fashions of 1864 and 1865. By the end of 1864, Mary was in mourning for her brother Levi; Mary's costume appears to be mourning attire.

Her jewelry consists of matching earrings, necklace, bracelets, and watch chain. They appears to have a black center (made from glass, onyx or other material) surrounded by small pearls. The dropped earrings clearly show Mary's pierced ears. The necklace consists of a strand of pearls and a center medallion or brooch. Her bracelets include the same medallion design as the necklace. Visible on her left hand is her simple wedding band and the diamond cluster ring that was given to her by President Lincoln.

Mary's headdress is a velvet band across the crown of her head, and a large bow lies at the back of the head. There is another band visible that may be a comb or the top of the snood, either of which serves the purpose of holding the hair in place.

The bodice has a long center point at the waist. Fashion plates of the era show many fashionable day bodices were "pointed in front with postillions behind which may be cut as several square basques and hang down to the knee level."[179] If it impossible to know if Mary's dress has postillions in the back. The finished edge of the bodice appears to be double piped.

A small braided trim is placed vertically on the sleeve, beginning at the shoulder seam and running to above the elbow. Pleated trim adorns the bodice sleeves and front in a shape intended to simulate a jacket. The skirt panels are gored, and some pleating is visible at the waist.

Black Silk with Trim, Circa 1864. (Photograph courtesy of The Lincoln Museum, Fort Wayne, IN (Reference #97) [identified as ML, O-23])

Throughout 1864 and 1865, it was popular for day dresses to be trimmed with "braiding, fringe, chenille, and grelots, mixed with jet, round the hem, up the sleeves, down the elbows, and on the cuffs and epaulettes."[180] Ruching and other frilling were often placed on the bodice to simulate a jacket shape. *Godey's* fashion plates show this style of costume in early 1864 and continue the fashion into 1865.

If Mary did wear this costume while in mourning for her brother, it is an excellent example of how, during her grief, she maintained a fashionable wardrobe within the mandates of social standards.

Day Dress with Open Skirt Circa 1864

The dress depicted in this engraving is a morning dress typical of the fashion which began its popularity towards the end of 1864. During 1865, costumes with an open skirt revealing the petticoat were highly fashionable.[181]

It is believed these engraving were made from a photograph taken by Matthew Brady.[182] The location of the original photograph is not known. One engraving shows Mary seated and facing right. The other is a composite artwork of the entire Lincoln family. The central figure of Abraham and Tad is based on a Brady photograph. Mary is posed just as she is in the engraving of just her; even the chair she sits in is the same. Robert, in his military uniform, stands behind his parents, and Willie's photograph hangs on the wall. Another lithograph created by Haskell & Allen in 1865, is also based on the Brady photographs.[183] In their work, the family circle is enlarged. Mary is placed across the table from Lincoln, and her image is reversed. Robert sits at the table beside his mother.

Mary's attire is a day robe with a high plain bodice. It has the typical hook-and-eye front closure. The dropped shoulder seams are decorated

Day Dress with Open Skirt, Circa 1864. (Engraving of Lincoln Family and engraving of Mary in dress with jockeys, CDV author's collection)

with jockeys trimmed with braid or ruching. The sleeves are full, but not as full as pagoda sleeves. The trim used on the jockeys is also used down the sleeve seam and around the sleeve cuff and down the bodice center front. White undersleeves are worn with the bodice. Narrow white linen collars were most appropriate with day bodices, and Mary wears a narrow white collar edged with scalloped lace. A small brooch holds the collar in place.

The skirt is open in the front from the waist to the hemline. The front edges are pulled up and attached to the skirt revealing a beautiful lining on the inside of the skirt. The front of the petticoat is visible. Mary's petticoat appears to be a solid color, and may be the same shade as the visible skirt lining. This was not always the case. *Godey's* fashion plates depict robes of this style in a variety of colors. Often the color of the trim matches the color of the petticoat. Some robes are made of a pale color fashion fabric and the skirt lining is a dark coordinating color. Some petticoats are white muslin with rows of inserted lace; some are decorated with contrasting ribbons or other trim.

Green and White Plaid Wrapper and Cape Circa 1864–1865

Mary's wrapper and matching cape are made of a green and white wool fabric. It consists of a day wrapper, a hip-length cape, collar, and belt. The garment is machine sewn except for hand stitching holding the belt firmly in place. The robe is a total of 60 inches in length at the center back and has a hemline circumference of 159 inches. These are typical measurements for daywear. The skirt appears to be circular cut with seams at the sides and the center front closure.

The bust measures forty inches and the waist measures forty-three

Green and White Plaid Wrapper
and Cape, Circa 1864–1865.
(Photos courtesy of the Chicago
History Museum)

inches, thus providing plenty of fabric for ease and comfort to the wearer. Wrappers were often worn at home or when a woman was doing manual labor; therefore, the extra ease in style allowed the wearer to move about more freely without the constraints of a fitted day bodice. The extra fullness is pulled in to the figure by the belt at the front: the waistline at the back and sides is closely fitted.

A two-inch-wide belt that is thirty inches in length is placed at the natural waistline. Patch pockets, angled and carefully matched to the grain of the skirt fabric, are ten inches wide and eight inches deep. Two buttons, matching others on the garment, and a black braid trim are located at the top of each pocket.

The round collar is trimmed with black braid and fastens with a large hook and eye and a large green button. Twenty-two one-inch black wool covered wooden buttons close the front of wrapper.

The garment has roomy two-piece coat-shaped sleeves twenty-four inches in length, which are trimmed with five rows of black braid at the cuff.

The cape is twenty-seven inches in length and has a hem measurement of 120 inches. It does not have a separate collar, and fastens with a center front button and a metal hook-and-eye closure.

Due to rigid mourning customs, we can deduce very closely when Mary wore this costume. The wrapper has construction details such as large patch pockets and coat sleeves which were popular in the winter months of 1864 and 1865. Woolen plaids were considered most fashionable in the winter of 1864 and a matching cape was popular in 1864 and 1865. Since Mary wore mourning in late 1864 and into January 1865, it is most likely she wore this morning costume in the early winter of 1865. And of course, Mary wore nothing but mourning after April 1865. This garment is in excellent condition. (Location: Chicago History Museum, Chicago, Illinois.)

Brocade Purple Silk
January 2, 1865

New Year's Day 1865 brought hope and celebration to Washington. General William T. Sherman's infamous march to the sea, which had begun in Atlanta, was completed. To notify the President that he had been successful, Sherman telegraphed Lincoln on Christmas Day and offered him the city of Savannah as a Christmas present. General Sheridan had successfully ended his four-month-long Shenandoah Campaign against Jubal Early in October. Only General Grant was still pursing the Confederate army. Richmond still stood as the Confederate capitol, and General Lee's forces were still fighting. But the end of the war was near.

The New Year's Day reception was postponed until January 2. At noon, President and Mrs. Lincoln received their guests with hope that peace would soon be restored throughout the nation. The first guests to enter were the diplomatic corps and the cabinet officers. At 12:30, the military officers and the Supreme Court justices entered. The general public was admitted at one o'clock, and by two, the jam was terrible.[184] Thousands of people came to shake the hand of the man who had led the nation through four years of turmoil and war. They had placed their trust in him during the November election with the hopes that he would now lead them in a time of peace and national healing.

Mrs. Lincoln stood beside her husband for hours. Her attire was described as a "heavy brocade purple silk, very richly trimmed with black velvet, over which was thrown a rich and exquisitely wrought black lace shawl."[185] The style of the dress is not described, but since the reception was held during the early afternoon, Mary would have worn a fashionably appropriate day dress.

The shape of the skirt changed at this time. Crinolines consisted of as many as thirty-five steel hoops; the upper part was slightly flattened. This was an effort to make the figure appear as slim as possible below the waist. Another effort to trim the waist line was the cut of the skirt's panels. They were gored, taking away the bulk of pleating the skirt. Every stylish lady knew that "the fewer pleats required around the waist, the more fashionable the dress."[186]

The style of Mary's bodice this particular day is not known, in general day bodices were plain and close fitting. It was common to wear a round linen collar and a velvet necktie. While it is doubtful that on such a special occasion Mary would have worn something considered common, she would have chosen something stylish.

Pearl with Lace
January 9, 1865

The first evening reception of the season was held at the Executive Mansion on January 9. 1865.

Little notice was made of Lincoln's attire for the evening. It was reported that he was "dressed in a plain suit of black, with white kid gloves."[187] Most likely, he wore several pairs of gloves that evening, putting on a clean, fresh pair of gloves as one pair became too soiled to offer to a lady's hand.

Mary's attire was given a little more notice than Lincoln's that evening, but still the description is vague. She wore a "rich dress of pearl color, heavily trimmed with the richest black lace, with a neat head-dress composed of a coronet of exquisite flowers."[188] Another source mentioned Mary's "necklace of pearls."[189]

The bodice for fashionable evening attire was "lower even if possible, than last season."[190] Both the bodice front and back were pointed. The front bodice fabric was pleated and arranged in a fan shape to a point in the center. The neckline was filled in with tulle puffing, an embroidered chemisette or worn with a bertha. Short sleeves had disappeared and were replaced with shoulder straps. The richest evening skirts had trains, and the double skirt was returning to fashion.

The President was especially weary this evening. He stopped receiving guests and retired for the evening at eleven.[191]

As President, there were many things that made Lincoln weary, and as a father and husband, a storm was brewing within the Lincoln family. Robert Lincoln wanted to join the army and serve his country. Lincoln did not want the people to think of his son as a shirker. He, himself, had served in the military during the Black Hawk War and knew that the discipline would mature Robert. Mary, on the other hand, was against Robert's enlisting. She had already buried two sons, and was nervous about the safety of her eldest son should he enlist. It was more than just his endangerment on the battlefield. There was also the question of what would happen if Robert were captured by the enemy. Mary was determined to keep Robert out of harm's way. When questioned by others, Mary defended her son, and explained the fault was her own. When asked by Senator Harris, in December 1863, why Robert had not enlisted, Mary replied, "If fault there be, it is mine, I have insisted that he should stay in college a little longer as I think an educated man can serve his country with more intelligent purpose than an ignoramus."[192] Now, with the war nearly over, and Robert's studies completed, Mary was out of excuses.

Black Corded Silk
January 21, 1865

On January 19, 1865, Lincoln wrote a letter to General Grant, not as his President but as his friend, requesting a position for Robert in the military. He wrote, "Could he [Robert], without embarrassment to you, or detriment to the service, go into your military family with some nominal rank, I, and not the public, furnishing his necessary means?"[193] Grant placed Robert Lincoln on his staff with the rank of captain. In that position, Robert was apparently out of harm's way, but his mother saw it differently.

Just a few days after Lincoln wrote his request to Grant, Mary held her usual Saturday afternoon reception. According to a Washington newspaper, "Mrs. Lincoln wore a very heavy black corded silk, elaborately trimmed, a shawl of white point lace, and a headdress composed of black velvet and lace."[194] This description suggests the dress was a mourning costume; in January Mary was still mourning her brother Levi.

Her demeanor was not mentioned; however, Mary would have graciously greeted her guests even when her heart was concerned for her son's safety.

Popular fashion plates for this season show day bodices with pointed fronts and one or more square basques in the back. Postillions vary in length and are often as long as knee-length. Fashion plates from *Godey's* show day bodices heavily trimmed with lace, braid, flutings, or fringe along the edges of the basques, sleeves, and bodice front. Often tassels, large ornamental buttons, or rosettes were placed at the center back at the level of the natural waistline.[195] Skirts were elliptical in shape, and petticoats were often trimmed with ruffles, flounces, and stripes.

Mary's black corded silk may not have had postillions or a basque, but it most surely was a current fashion.

Black Velvet
March 4, 1865

At times, it was doubtful that Lincoln would win the election of 1864. Even Mary, who always supported her husband's political career, had her doubts. When he was reelected, she was relieved. Mary had accumulated a great debt, and her husband did not know. As the wife of the President, she could keep the creditors at bay a little longer.

A platform had been erected in front of the central portico of the Capitol Building for the inaugural ceremony on Saturday, March 4, 1865. Senator James Harlan from Iowa served as Mary's escort to the ceremonies. A little after noon, Abraham Lincoln, dressed in a black suit, placed his hand on the Bible, and took the Presidential Oath for the second time. As Samuel Chase held the Bible, Lincoln leaned forward and kissed it. Mr. Chase then presented the Bible to Mary. Very little has been said of Mary Lincoln's attire as she stood on the platform beside her husband. Her dress was described as "black velvet trimmed with ermine. She was dressed with great elegance, and was the center of attraction."[196]

Light Drab
March 4, 1865

Around eight P.M. the "White House gates were thrown open and several thousand persons made a grand rush to enter is portal to attend the inaugural reception. President and Mrs. Lincoln received their guests with graceful cordiality."[197] It was the largest reception of the season. Approximately six thousand people came and shook hands with the President. It was reported that Mrs. Lincoln was attired in a "light drab dress with an overdress of lace."[198]

White Silk Satin with Lace
March 6, 1865

The inaugural ball was postponed until Monday, March 6. It was held in the "great hall of the handsome, neoclassical Patent Office with the

American flag playing a predominant part in the decorations." Admission tickets for the ball were ten dollars — a rather costly amount for the era. People were happy to pay it for the proceeds were slated to go to a fund for the widows and children of soldiers who had been killed in battle.[199]

Three bands entertained the crowd that evening. The opening promenade began at ten P.M. Upon the Lincolns' arrival (sometime between ten and eleven) the military band struck up "Hail to the Chief" and Lincoln was escorted down the center of the hall by Speaker of the House Schuyler Colfax of Indiana. Mrs. Lincoln was escorted by Senator Charles Sumner of Massachusetts.[200] Robert Lincoln attended the ball with Mary, the daughter of Iowan Senator James Harlan.

On March 7, *The New York Times* said very little of Mary and her attire at the inaugural ball. They simply reported, "Mrs. Lincoln is most richly dressed in a white moiré antique, profusely ornamented with exquisite lace."[201] The editors must have felt that readers needed more information about Mary's dress, for the next day a much longer description of Mary's gown was printed along with a mention of the President:

> He wore a plain black suit and white gloves. Mrs. Lincoln looked extremely well and was attired in the most elegant manner; her dress was made of white satin, very ample and rich but almost entirely covered by a tunic or rather skirt of the finest "point appliqué." Her corsage, which was low, and short sleeves were ornamented richly by a bertha made of the same material, and the shawl, also of the same rich lace, was most exquisite "passementerie" of narrow fluted satin ribbons and "boucle" completed the dress. Her jewels were of the rarest pearls, necklace, ear rings, brooch, and bracelets. Her hair, which was put plainly back from her face, was ornamented with trailing Jessamine and clustering violets most gracefully. She looked exceedingly well with her soft white complexion, and her toilet was faultless. Her manners were easy and affable.[202]

Another source states that Mary carried "an ermine fan with silver spangles."[203]

A few months later, Mary was a widow and deeply in debt. She tried to raise funds by selling this dress. The dress was costly, and Mary needed help finding a buyer with deep pockets and sympathy towards her. On August 31, 1865, she wrote to her dear friend Sally Orne hoping to find a buyer for the dress and some unmade fabric. Mary described her situation and the articles:

> If my darling husband had lived out, his four years, he promised me, we should pass our remaining years, in a home, we both should have enjoyed. We are left, with only $1500 — a year, each, to live upon, the interest on our money, and as a matter of course, must board, plainly and as genteel as possible, on this sum. I mention this, by way of excusing a subject, I will mention to you. A friend of my husband's & myself, presented me last February, a *very* elegant lace dress, very fine & beautiful — lace flounce about 6 inches, in width, for the bottom of the skirt — same pattern as dress — a double lace shawl, very fine, exactly similar pattern, with the request, that I would wear it, on the night of the Inauguration — for two hours, that evening, I did so, over a white silk dress, next morning, most carefully, the *gathers* were drawn from the skirt — and it was folded *tenderly* away — the flounce, was not used. I wore the article, reluctantly, as it was too elaborate for my style & too expensive, for my means — My desire is, to dispose of these articles, it cost, in New York, to import them $3,500 — of course — if I can get $2,500 — for them, it will be a great consideration to me. If you know, of any one, who would desire, such a dress, will you not gratify me, my dear friend, by informing me. You may well be assured, only *dire* necessity, which I have never before, known, anything, about — would cause me to write so freely to you. The lace dress && is exquisitely fine, and was considered,

a bargain at the $3,500. I have also — the most magnificent white moiré antique that Mr. Stewart says, he ever had imported — it was purchased last winter & never made up — $11 a yard — a yard wide. Some 16 yards in the dress I would sell at $125 — I am so anxious to have my boys, in a quiet home of our own — & without I make some exertions of the kind, disposing of my articles, now unnecessary, I fear, I can not succeed. If any of your friends would desire such articles, please advise me — they are rich & beautiful.[204]

Evidently, Mrs. Orne was unsuccessful in helping Mary find a buyer for the dress. A few years later, this gown was listed among others that Mary wished to sell during her Old Clothes Scandal in New York City.

Black and White Dress, Black Velvet Cloak, and White Silk Bonnet April 14, 1865 — Good Friday

What should have been a joyous night of entertainment and celebration turned into one of the darkest nights for the Lincoln family and the entire nation. The previous week, General Robert E. Lee surrendered his troops to General Ulysses S. Grant. Robert Lincoln was present during the historic meeting at Appomattox Courthouse, Virginia. After four long years of bloodshed, of brother fighting brother, and over 600,000 deaths, the war was over. The people of Washington City were celebrating and looking forward to the future.

It was business as usual at the White House on April 14. Robert arrived home in time to have breakfast with his father. After a pleasant breakfast, President Lincoln met with several members of Congress and later held a cabinet meeting. Between two and three that afternoon he took a break from is official duties to have lunch with Mary and then returned to his office for a meeting with Vice-President Johnson. His afternoon was filled with more appointments. In the late afternoon, Lincoln and his wife took a carriage ride and visited the Navy Yard.[205]

In November 1865, Mary shared her memories of the carriage ride and other personal moments in a letter written to Francis Bicknell Carpenter:

> How I wish you could have seen my dear husband, the last three weeks of his life! Having a realizing sense, that the unnatural rebellion was near its close, & being most of the time, *away* from W, where he had endured such conflicts of mind, within the last four years, feeling *so encouraged*, he freely gave vent to his cheerfulness. Down the Potomac, he was almost boyish, in his mirth & reminded me, of his original nature, what I had always remember of him, in our own home — free from care, surrounded by those he loved so well & *by whom*, he was so idolized. *The Friday*, I never saw him so supremely cheerful — his manner was even playful. At three o'clock, in the afternoon, he drove out with me in the open carriage, in starting I asked him, if any one, should accompany us, he immediately replied — "No — I prefer to ride by ourselves to day." During the drive he was so gay, that I said to him, laughingly, "Dear Husband, you almost startle me by your great cheerfulness," he replied, "and well I may feel so, Mary, I consider *this day*, the war, has come to a close — and then added, "We must *both*, be more cheerful in the future — between the war & the loss of our darling Willie — we have both been very miserable.[206]

Although Mary made a mistake in reference to the time of the carriage ride (Lincoln's meeting with Johnson was held at three o'clock) she undoubtedly remembered the sentiment of the ride correctly.

The Lincolns returned from their carriage ride between six and seven P.M. and found Illinois Governor Richard J. Oglesby and other friends

118

Black Silk Dress, 1861
(see pages 59–61)

Sadly, several years ago this dress was displayed in a sunlit window and is now severely damaged. The colors are faded on the right side of the dress, and in many places the fabric is cracked and fragile. The dress has been stabilized by a conservator, yet it remains too fragile for permanent display. (Location: ALPL, Springfield, Illinois.)

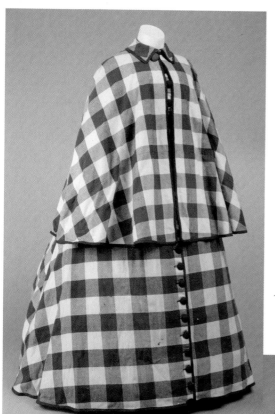

Green and White Plaid Wrapper and Cape, Circa 1864–1865 (see pages 107–109)

Wrappers were often worn at home or when a woman was doing manual labor; therefore, the extra ease in style allowed the wearer to move about more freely without the constraints of a fitted day bodice. The extra fullness is pulled in to the figure by the belt at the front: the waistline at the back and sides is closely fitted. (Photos courtesy of the Chicago History Museum)

Black and White Dress, Black Velvet Cloak, and White Silk Bonnet, April 14, 1865 — Good Friday. (Photographs of black velvet cloak, bonnet, and scrap of silk fabric courtesy of Chicago History Museum)

from their home state waiting for them at the White House. After a brief visit and a quick supper, the President met with Congressman Colfax of Indiana.

The President, Mary, and their guests Major Henry R. Rathbone and his fiancée, Miss Clara Harris, entered Ford's Theatre that evening around 8:30. The play was a comedy titled *Our American Cousin*, and starred Laura Keene. Theatre attendees that evening noticed that both Abraham and Mary enjoyed the play. Mary "seemed to take great pleasure in witnessing his enjoyment."[207] Lincoln sat in a rocking chair, and Mary sat in a chair next to him. Their hands were clasped together and Mary was leaning on his shoulder. They were happy. Mary turned to Lincoln and softly asked, "What will Miss Harris think of my hanging on to you so?" Lincoln smiled and gently replied, "She won't think any thing about it."[208]

When a lone actor was on stage, and when he had just uttered one of the funniest lines in the script, John Wilkes Booth moved into the Presidential box. A shot rang out, and most of the audience thought the sound was part of the play. Mary was still nestled against her husband when she heard the sound. She never said what exactly made her realize her husband had been wounded — a look on his face, a jerk of his hand, maybe his hand letting go of hers. It was her agonizing screams that alerted the audience that the President had been assassinated.

The next few minutes were wild pandemonium. Booth had managed to slice open Major Rathbone's arm, leap onto the stage and run out the back door. A doctor was lifted into the President's viewing box. It was decided the President should be moved. Several men carried him across the street into the home of William Petersen. Lincoln was placed on a bed in a small room on the ground floor. In the confusion of crossing the street, Mary, who was escorted by Major Rathbone, became separated from her husband. Major Rathbone's arm was bleeding, and he needed medical attention as well. Someone sent for Robert, and he and John Hay (one of Lincoln's secretaries) arrived. Once he arrived at the Peterson house, Robert was told that his father's wound was fatal and there was no hope of survival. Throughout the night family, friends, and government officials came to wait for the inevitable.

During the night, Mary tried to stay near her husband. Her grief overcame her and she called out for Lincoln to live. She could not imagine life without him. Whenever her wails became too loud, or she could not control her emotions, she would leave the small room and sit in the parlor. As Lincoln's breath became more rattled, Mary became more unnerved and frightened. In one loud series of death rattles, Mary cried out and fainted. Secretary of War Edwin Stanton ordered, "Take that woman out and do not let her in again!"[209] It was the last time Mary saw her beloved husband.

As Mary left the room to return to the parlor, a reporter overheard her say, "Oh, my God, and have I given my husband to die."[210] At 7:22 A.M., Lincoln slipped through the "thin veil" that Victorians believed separated the living and the lost. When the doctor pronounced the President dead, Reverend Phineas Densmore Gurley stepped forward and began to pray. James Tanner, who was taking notes of the death watch, reported that Secretary Stanton said, "He belongs to the angels now." Others who were present recalled Stanton's comment as, "Now he belongs to the ages."[211]

With Lincoln's death, the nation was plunged into a deep mourning. Easter Sunday became "Black Sunday." The massive white floral displays, which traditionally decorated the altars of churches throughout the nation, were replaced with black mourning crape. Christian leaders from all denominations began to introduce "the mystical connections that linked Lincoln's death to the original Good Friday martyrdom in Judea."[212]

As the news of Lincoln's death spread, people began to visit every spot associated with their fallen President. Some people were content with a glimpse of various buildings and rooms associated with Lincoln. Curious souvenir seekers came to the same places looking for an artifact. Wallpaper was stripped from walls, curtains were cut, and carpets were pulled to bits.

Newspapers were quick to print stories about Lincoln's assassination and the events which followed. The people clamored for every detail. For the second time since coming to Washington, national news dominated and Mary Lincoln's attire was not mentioned in any of the press releases. Following her nature, Mary gave away the clothing worn by her and her husband that night, for the sight of it was too painful for her.

Lincoln's overcoat, frock coat and trousers were given to Alphonso Donn, the White House doorman. Other relics were found by various persons and were not returned to Mary. Willie Clark, the boarder at the Petersen House whose room was used as a makeshift hospital for the injured President, kept Lincoln's boots. Lincoln's hat was found in the box at Ford's theatre and given to the police. His cane was found and kept by an actor.[213]

Mrs. Keckley recalled that Mary gave her dress to "Mrs. Slade, the wife of an old and faithful messenger." She continued, "The cloak, stained with the President's blood was given to me, as also was the bonnet worn on the same memorable night."[214] Today, these garments, or in some cases, what is left of these garments are preserved in historical archives.

The Dress

The swatch of fabric from the dress allegedly worn to Ford's Theatre by Mary Lincoln is a black silk taffeta with small white floral sprays. The flowers are spaced about two inches apart.

The style of the dress is unknown. Since the Presidential party traveled to the theatre by carriage, and there were not changing rooms for them after they arrived, it is likely Mary wore a type of carriage dress or dinner dress. This would have been more stylish than something she would have worn at home in the White House, but not as elaborate as something worn to a formal White House dinner, reception, or ball.

Godey's fashion plates show several costumes which would have been appropriate to wear to the theatre. Tight bodices and sleeves were fashionable. Fashion plates show matching trims made from ruching, fringe, cording, or quilling on both the bodice and the skirt. Since the fabric has a floral design, the dress trim would probably have been made either from the same fabric or perhaps a solid black or white silk.

Some costumes have a skirt made "en tablier", with an apron-shaped panel down the front, and edged with fluted ruffles. The bodice may be trimmed with a fluted ruffle to give the illusion of a jacket and also have a deep basque at the back waist, edged with the same fluted ruffle.

Which ever style of dress Mary chose for this evening, it was exquisite. She took great care to see that all of the garments in her costume coordinated. The two garments which have survived are examples of the highest quality, richest materials, and talented craftsmanship that was available at the time.

The Cloak

When Mary walked into Ford's Theatre and took her place in the Presidential box, the audience did not see her dress, but this elegant evening cloak.

The outer part of the cloak is made from black silk velvet. The lining is quilted black silk taffeta with a cotton batting. Both silk and cotton thread were used to make this garment. It is full-length, coming to just three or four inches above the hem of the dress, circular in cut, and has fitted shoulders.

The arm holes have been sewn shut, most likely for storage purposes. A black lace medallion surrounds each arm hole. A rosette is located at the top and bottom of each opening, and a small braid trim runs down the opening. It is not clear if this braid trim is original to the garment or not.

Instead of a collar, the neckline is finished with cording made of three strands, two white and one black. At the end of each cord is a huge decorative tassel made with wooden pieces covered in fabric, cords, and threads. The tassel begins with a vase shaped piece covered in white silk fabric and black decorative threads. Next is a disk covered in a fuzzy white material. The next piece is covered in white silk and decorated in the same black thread used in the large first piece. Hanging down from the white covered disk are four white cords with black velvet. Suspended from each cord is a small white tassel.

The Bonnet

The bonnet that Mary Lincoln allegedly wore to Ford's Theatre is covered in white silk satin. The bonnet brim is decorated with a dainty white lace that is tipped with a black edging. The top of the brim is filled with velvet leaves, seed pods, and beads. One large black velvet maple leaf is located on the top right edge, directly above the wear's eyebrow. This is followed by a cluster of black beads. White seed pods have one dangling bead in the center surrounded by six small beads. These are followed by three velvet covered wires.

The outside of the brim is covered with white silk that is quilted in half-inch squares. The crown is draped with white silk that has four folds of fabric. The bonnet skirt is made from black velvet, two inches in width. A one inch band of black ribbon is located on the skirt and it appears there had once been a black velvet bow attached.

Inside the bonnet is finished with white silk and a white net is sewn into the very back. One inch wide, white satin ties complete the bonnet. (Location: Chicago History Museum, Chicago Illinois)

Black Merino Dress 1867

Mary remained in the White House for forty days after the assassination. She secluded herself in the upstairs quarters and could not gather enough composure to attend her husband's funeral. At a time when she most needed rest, comfort, and understanding, she was thrown into one of the most bitter fights of her life — that of the final resting place for her beloved husband. Shortly after Lincoln's death, former friends, neighbors, and colleagues in Illinois formed the National Lincoln Monument Association. Their purpose was to purchase property in downtown Springfield and erect a moment and vault for the slain

President. There was only one small problem: no one discussed it with Mary. She was livid.

During a walk through a peaceful secluded graveyard, Lincoln had said to his wife, "Mary, you are younger than I. You will survive me. When I am gone, lay my remains in some quiet place like this."[215] Mary wanted Abraham buried in Oak Ridge Cemetery and a tomb built that would also allow space for her, her children and their families. For months, the two sides bickered over the details. Finally, Mary wrote to Illinois Governor Richard J. Oglesby in June 1865, "If I had anticipated, so much trouble, in having my wishes carried out, I should have readily yielded to the request of the *many* & had *his* precious remains, in the *first instance* placed in a vault of the National Capitol — A tomb prepared for Washington the Father of his Country & a fit resting place for the immortal Savior & Martyr for Freedom."[216] The battle was over, and Mary had won.

When the remaining members of the Lincoln family moved to Chicago, life was drastically different for them. At first the family of three lived in an apartment at the Tremont House. But they could only afford to live there for one week. As the new male head of the household, it became Robert's responsibility to find suitable and affordable living arrangements for the family. He chose an apartment of three rooms in the resort community of Hyde Park.

Mary observed the rules of mourning and mostly stayed in their small rented rooms trying to remain as far removed from society as possible. She rarely ventured into the city streets, received few callers, and called on no one. At this time in her life, Mary undoubtedly cared nothing about fashion.

Slowly, Mary did begin to receive visitors and venture out into the Chicago stores. She felt that people were looking at her clothing and making comments. And, they probably were, for to the Victorian's appearance was everything. In Mary's case, her appearance as a properly dressed widow helped bolster Lincoln's memory. If "the clothes make the man," in this case, the widow's clothes make the memory.

To be dressed in out of date fashions was unthinkable to someone like Mary. People would stare and speak in hushed tones to see one of Mary's former social status inappropriately dressed walking in the social districts or stores of places like Chicago and New York. It was with this in mind that Mary wrote to Lizzie Keckley in December 1867:

> I am positively suffering for a decent dress. I see Mr. A. [unidentified] and *some* recent visitors eyeing my clothing askance . . . Do send my black merino dress to me very soon; I must dress better in the future.[217]

Since Lizzie was still in New York overseeing the sale of Mary's belongings at the time this letter was written this particular dress may have been one already made and in storage. More likely though, it was a new dress. From the tone of Mary's letters to Lizzie, it seems that Lizzie was complaining about her personal lack of funds. Mary had written asking her if she could find some sewing work in New York while she continued to oversee the clothing sale. In October 1865, Mary wrote to said that Lizzie would not recognize her and that "the glass shows me a pale, wretched, haggard face, and my dresses are like bags on me."[218] It is most probable that in order to help Lizzie finically, and to have less people eyeing her clothing askance, Mary needed a new dress.

The fashions of 1867 were quite different from those earlier in the decade. Much older styles were revived and modernized. The empire waistline, with a "high waisted bodice attached, high neck, tight sleeves, and trimming of velvet to simulate a tunic" became a popular style of walking dress. Another fashionable walking dress was "looped-up at the sides to reveal a bright colored petticoat." In general, the bulk of a skirt was moved further to the rear of the garment, thus beginning the era of the bustle.[219]

Bodices were made plain and high with tightly fitted coat sleeves. Sashes and large bows decorated the waistline. *Godey's* fashion plates reveal costumes with overdresses, double skirts, sacque and petticoat costumes, and dresses with matching coats. Of course, Mary would have admired many of the trims and fancier costumes, but would not have worn them in her widowhood. Her own dresses would be made with the same shape as fashionable dresses, but without the frills.

Old Clothes Scandal
1867

According to Elizabeth Keckley, when packing to leave the White House for Chicago, Mary turned to her and said, "Lizzie, I may see the day when I shall be obliged to sell a portion of my wardrobe. If Congress does not do something for me, then my dresses some day may have to go to bring food into my mouth, and the mouths of my children."[220] The garments were of no interest to Mary since she was a widow who planned to wear mourning for the rest of her life. Her White House wardrobe was made from the finest materials and just sitting in trunks. If sold, Mary could invest the money and earn a modest income from the interest.

She had petitioned Congress to award her the one hundred thousand-dollar salary her husband would have made as President over the four years of his second term. Instead, she was award twenty-five thousand dollars, or one year's salary. Most of this was used to purchase and furnish a home in Chicago. Mary was receiving interest from her savings and a regular check for the rent on the home in Springfield, but she needed additional income to pay her bills. Mary felt that she needed additional income to feel secure in caring for her own needs, as well as for her fourteen-year-old son Tad.

In September 1867 Mary's words to Lizzie became reality. The two women met in New York and together they enlisted the services of Brady & Company, located at 609 Broadway to sell Mary's wardrobe. Mary used the assumed name of "Mrs. Clark." She wanted to remain incognito, but Mr. Brady and his associate Mr. Keyes convinced Mary that if her identity and her financial needs were made known to the public, a handsome sum could be raised. The garments were soon displayed at Brady's store, but the result was not what Mr. Brady and Mr. Keyes had expected.

Articles began to appear in newspapers across the country with titles such "Disgraceful," "Something to Wear," and "Disrespectfully Dedicated to Mrs. Abraham Lincoln." One newspaper reporter expressed the sentiments of many when he wrote:

> . . . Mrs. Lincoln is now in New York City, under the assumed name of Mrs. Clark, peddling out her clothes to the highest bidder. . . . We have seen a list of the articles she offers for sale — It embraces nearly or quite every article of known female wear, from fine Cashmere shawls down to her old stockings and drawers. Many of the fine shawls, dresses, diamonds, rings, bracelets, necklaces &c., were presents to her from the admirers of her husband — such articles as are usually kept as souvenirs. Some are ungracious enough to say that they were presented for the purpose of obtaining her influence with her husband to get a fat office. It may be true. If it is, it shows the natural disposition of the "live Yankee" to take advantage of all circumstances, however despicable. . . . But seriously, of the many low, sordid, ill-bred exhibitions our country has made, we think this is the most infamous. For the widow of the President of the United States who has a magnificent fortune for her support, to be peddling her old clothes, through the country, for fear they will get out of fashion, is almost too much. We commend the spectacle to the admirers of "the late lamented."[221]

All of the former accusations made against Mary during the Presidential years were in the newspapers again with more tales added to the media circus. Her loyalties during the war were again questioned by members of the press. Mary was accused of stealing furniture and other bits of government property from the White House. A Northern newspaper explained Mary's prolonged forty-day stay at the White House after Lincoln's death as a trick she derived by pretending to be pregnant in order to have more time to pack up valuables. A Southern newspaper claimed that Mary was about to marry again.[222] In addition to lists of her clothing and accusations against her, *The New York World* published private letters Mary had written to Mr. Brady.

It was more than Robert could bear. He was furious with his mother for publicly humiliating the family. He became frantic, and was quoted as saying the only explanation for his mother's behavior and her plans to sell her wardrobe was that she was insane.[223] Robert was a young attorney with his own professional and personal reputation to protect. Victorian society required the male head of the household, whether he was the husband, father, or the eldest son, to care for, protect, and control the women in the family. Although he was a young man of only twenty-five years of age, the responsibilities were nevertheless his. A public scandal reflected poorly upon his ability to manage his household and could affect his professional career.

Mary felt betrayed by Mr. Brady because of the horrid publicity; she felt abandoned by her husband's political friends who seemed to not care if she had a home or not, and her heart was broken that her son felt so upset and humiliated. On October 6, 1867, Mary wrote to Lizzie Keckley:

> I am writing this morning with a broken heart after a sleepless night of great mental suffering. R[obert] came up last evening like a maniac, because the letters of the *World* were published in yesterday's paper. I could not refrain from weeping when I saw him so miserable. But yet, my dear good Lizzie, was it not to protect myself and help others — and was not my motive and action of the purest kind? Pray for me that this cup of affliction may pass from me, or be sanctified to me . . . Only my darling Taddie prevents my taking my life . . .[224]

The sale was unsuccessful in all respects. Mr. Brady and Mr. Keyes planned to exhibit the wardrobe in Providence, in hopes of raising money for Mary and selling more of the articles. However, when Mr. Brady arrived, the city authorities would not allow the exhibition. Mr. Brady returned to New York with the clothing. Robert began to seriously doubt his mother's mental well-being, and the general public's opinion of Mary was blackened.

While the clothing was displayed at Brady's store, newspapers began to report stories about the condition of the clothing. Curiosity seekers came to look and to touch the garments but did not come to make any purchases. The clothing was laid about on tables, thrown over the backs of chairs, and hung on pegs on the walls. Mary was appalled. Fearing that her garments were "getting pulled to pieces and soiled," Mary wrote to Mrs. Keckley requesting her to have "the finest articles packed up and returned," among which were:

Single white camel's hair shawl
Two paisley shawls, white
1 camel's hair shawl — double black center
1 camel's hair shawl, double white center
1 pair bracelets and ear rings
1 Fine lace handkerchief
3 black lace shawls
2 black lama shawls
1 dress, silk, unmade, white and black
1 white boa
1 Russian sable boa
1 Russian sable cape
1 A. sable cape, cuffs, and muff
1 Chinchilla set
The lace dress, flounce and shawl[225]

Newspaper descriptions of the sale give more information about the garments. There were three beautiful brocade dresses simply thrown on a table. The dress worn at Lincoln's second inauguration was treated more carefully. It was placed in a box and brought out on request. One source describes this outfit as originally costing forty-two hundred dollars in gold (not paper currency) and consisting of skirt, handkerchief, flounces, and a parasol cover. (Oddly, no bodice was mentioned.) They were a bargain at the asking price of two thousand dollars.[226] Another newspaper reported this set include a white point lace shawl, dress, flounce, parasol cover, and handkerchief, and was valued at nearly forty-five hundred dollars.[227] These were considered huge sums of money. Just two years before, *Peterson's Magazine* had advertised a three-story suburban residence complete with modern water closets for slightly over four thousand dollars.

Other items of interest mentioned in the newspapers were Mary's shawls and her jewelry. The lists included:

Five elegant camel's hair shawls which were tossed across the
   back of a chair —
One long shawl with a black center, valued at $1,500
One long shawl with a white center, valued at $1,200
One square shawl with a white center, valued at $400
One square shawl with a black center, valued at $350
One square shawl with a red center, valued at $100
Two white Paisley shawls lie on the lounger,
   valued at $300 each
One long Paisley shawl, valued at $75
One square Paisley shawl, valued at $50 (may be the same ones
   mentioned on the lounger)

There is some discrepancy over the number of shawls at the sale. One newspaper reported seven heavy point lace shawls, total value four thousand dollars; while another newspaper mentioned six shawls total — five black and one white.[228]

A Russian sable cape, noted to be made from the finest and softest fur, was priced at fifteen hundred dollars. Other furs included a Russian sable boa; sable cape, cuffs, and muff; and a white boa. It was noted that twenty-three dresses, valued at ten thousand dollars, were piled in a heap on a table.

A few pieces of Mary's jewelry were also noted by member of the press:

Two elaborately wrought bracelets of the finest gold,
    valued at $800
Diamond pin and earrings made from rare, large stones,
    valued at $1,500
Two smaller diamond rings, valued at $350 and $500
Solitaire diamond earrings, valued at $300
Watch and chain, valued at $1,000

At the conclusion of the sale on March 4, 1868, Mary closed her accounts with Brady & Company, and the following items were returned to her:

One trunk	1 set of furs
1 lace dress	2 paisley shawls
1 lace dress, flounced	2 gold bracelets
5 lace shawls	16 dresses
3 camel hair shawls	2 Opera cloaks
1 lace parasol cover	1 purple shawl
1 dozen handkerchiefs	1 feather cape
1 sable boa	28 yards silk[229]
1 white boa	

According to Elizabeth Keckley, the following items were also sold during the sale:

1 diamond ring	1 red shawl
3 small rings	2 dresses
1 set of furs	1 child's shawl
1 camel hair shawl	1 lace Chantilly shawl

Record-keeping for this sale may have been mishandled. While some items do appear in the newspapers and are again mentioned in Mary's letters, many items are not mentioned in both texts. The number of shawls is questionable. The list of sold items does not offer sufficient descriptions to identify each item. And there does not seem to be any record of who purchases which items.

The failed sale had been a personal and financial blow to Mary. Her letters indicate that she was depressed over the publicity and humiliated by the scandal. In some ways, she viewed the lack of sales and support as personal betrayals. Soon, Mary was to feel betrayed again — this time by Elizabeth Keckley. Mary had given Lizzie the cloak and bonnet that she wore to Ford's Theatre that fatal night. Lizzie in turn donated the items to Wilberforce College where her son had received his education. The college had suffered a great fire the same day that Lincoln was assassinated, and Lizzie donated the garments for them to do with as they wished. Their plan was to tour the garments throughout Europe in order to raise funds for the school. Mary was horrified when she learned of this plan. She wrote to Lizzie:

> Your letter announcing that my clothes were to be paraded in Europe — those I gave you — has almost turned me wild. R[obert] would go raving distracted if such a thing was done.[230]

The college decided not to parade Mary's cloak and bonnet throughout Europe. Most likely the change in plan was done at Lizzie's request.

Mary had promised to pay Lizzie for her time and efforts for helping with the sale of the wardrobe. After all, she had closed up her shop in Washington for the opportunity to help Mary and make money herself. With little sales and failure to raise funds, Mary was not able to pay Lizzie as she had planned. The Old Clothes Sale was over, but there was still more scandal to come.

Needing money, Mrs. Keckley remained in New York with friends. Just ten days after the end of the business with Brady's, Lizzie wrote and

Old Clothes Sale, 1867. (Engraving, Courtesy of the ALPLM, Springfield, IL)

signed the preface to her book, *Behind the Scenes: Thirty Years a Slave, and Four Years in the White House*. The first part of the book was Lizzie's story of being born into slavery, buying her freedom, and coming to Washington to sew for the political powerhouses of the nation. The bulk of the book was about the personal and private lives of the Lincolns in the White House. Lizzie had to understand that some would see her book as gossipy or as a betrayal of trust. In her preface she wrote, "If I have betrayed confidence in anything I have published, it has been to place Mrs. Lincoln in a better light before the world. A breach of trust — if breach it can be called — of this kind is excusable."[231]

The public reaction to the book was not completely positive. Some people believed it was a breech of trust for a servant to write about the inner sanctuary of the home. Lizzie included her own opinions about members of the Lincoln family, dialogue from overheard conversations, and letters in their entirety. Some even questions whether Lizzie wrote the book herself, or whether it was ghostwritten. She answered that question herself several years later during a newspaper interview. Lizzie explained the composition of her book by saying that she "told her story to two newspapermen who employed stenographers, got what she said down in writing, and published it."[232] She explained further that her goals were to present Mary in a positive manner, to explain why she sold her wardrobe, and to make money. She accomplished none of her goals at a huge personal cost to Mary.

If Robert suffered humiliation from Mary's actions, this book caused him even more pain. Mary was furious with Lizzie for her involvement with the book. The two never saw one another or communicated with one another again. Mary's circle of friends and supporters continued to grow smaller.

Widow's Attire
September 24, 1868

In years past when Mary Lincoln had appeared in public, the press usually printed a record of her attire. This day she was in Washington City wearing a deep mourning costume. Nothing was written about Mary's dress other than it was a "plain black" one.[233]

It was the first time Mary had traveled to Washington since the death of her husband. The city had too many painful for memories to return for a visit. But this day was about making new, positive memories. Robert Todd Lincoln was to marry Mary Eunice Harlan.

Victorian customs said it was bad luck for a widow to attend a wedding in mourning attire. Most widows put aside their mourning for the day, and returned to it after the festivities were completed. If they could not put the mourning attire aside, social etiquette allowed a widow to attend a wedding in absentia. She attended, but sat away from the other guests and did not attend any of the social festivities associated with the wedding. Mary could not bear to put her mourning aside; she attended her son's wedding in absentia.

Plain Black Silk
April 4, probably prior to 1868

Little has been recorded about Mary's clothing throughout her widowhood. She lived mostly in solitude; few visitors wrote about their encounters with the widow of Abraham Lincoln, and even fewer commented about her attire. Benjamin Moran of the American legation in London made a journal entry describing Mary's "excellent manners" and her "deep black dress and widow's cap."[234] Most accounts, if they mentioned Mary's attire at all, simply noted that she wore deep mourning. As a woman who had loved fashion and colors all of her life, Mary's commitment to remain in mourning after Lincoln's death was a testament to the depth of her grief for her husband. Never did she complain about the blackness of her crape or the plainness of her garments.

A friend and journalist, Jane Grey Swisshelm, wrote of Mary's widow's attire:

> With all her love of beautiful garments, and the cultivation of that love as a patriotic duty, no woman ever sustained the dignity of widowhood by more appropriate demeanor. Only once did she lay aside her heavy weeds, and this at the earnest entreaty of her son, Tad, on the occasion of his birthday, when she wore a plain black silk dress."[235]

This dress would have been void of jewelry, shiny buttons, and other adornments. Mary may have chosen to wear a white collar or cuffs instead of those made from the deepest black crape. The plain, black silk dress would have been an appropriate mourning costume. According to Mrs. Swisshelm, Mary set "aside her heavy weeds," but did not cast off her mourning altogether.

Popular culture has made more of this story than is truly known. Movies, plays, and historical novels often tell the story of how Tad was ill on his eighteenth birthday and begged his mother to wear something other than black to cheer him. Mary, rising to the occasion, pulled the inaugural ball gown from 1861 out of her trunks and wore it for the day.[236] This did not happen.

Mother and son were in London for Tad's eighteenth birthday. There is no recorded evidence of Mary's choice of costume for that day, but it is unlikely that she was hauling the 1861 inaugural dress throughout Europe since most of her belongings were in storage back home in the United States. Whether or not Mary still had possession of this dress is questionable. The dress she wore at the 1865 inaugural was at the Old Clothes Sale; it is reasonable to believe that the 1861 inaugural gown was there as well.

White Silk Skirt
1871

Worn when Mary Lincoln was presented to the court at St. James Palace in England, this skirt nearly met the same tragic end as its bodice.

While living and traveling throughout Europe, Mary and Tad spent time in London, England. Sometime during their stay, Mary received an invitation to be presented at court. At Tad's request, Mary did not wear her traditional mourning attire that day. Instead, she had a gown of white silk and coral fashioned for the event. Since the bodice of the gown no longer exists, it is impossible to determine exactly what it looked like. The polonaise costume was in vogue and it is possible this gown was of that style. Made with a longer bodice, a polonaise gown would have been considered appropriate court dress.

Mary gave the dress to Louisa Todd, her niece, (the youngest daughter of her elder brother Levi Todd). Louisa wore it on October 10, 1876, when she married Edwards Keyes of Springfield, Illinois. Family members also recalled Louisa saying that she had the dress made into a dancing skirt.[237] By the time of Mary's death, the dress had found its way into a box and was stored in Louisa's attic. Having only sons, and no daughter to pass the dress to, Louisa did not have any future plans for the gown. In her golden years, Louisa could be found on her front porch with this dress by her side. As strangers passed by, Louisa would call out and ask them if they would like to have a piece of a dress once worn by Mary Lincoln. If the response was affirmative, Louisa took her scissors, cut off a piece of the bodice and presented it to the waiting hands of a stranger. She managed to give away the entire bodice bit by bit. A rectangular hole in the skirt shows where Louisa's scissors had begun their damaging work there as well.

White Silk Skirt, 1871. (Photograph by Jim Helm courtesy of Abraham Lincoln Presidential Library & Museum (ALPLM) Springfield, IL)

The skirt is made of white satin twill and is fully lined with white chintz. The four-panel skirt is thirty-eight inches in length with a hem circumference of eighty inches. The gored center front panel has a top width of nine inches. The two gored side panels are basically five inches in width at the waistline with the right-side panel being slightly larger due to the eleven-inch-deep placket opening. The back panel is a straight panel. It has had the pleating removed so a finished measurement is difficult to determine. The unfinished measurement is twenty-three inches. Inside the waistline, there is evidence of several inches of cartridge pleating at the center back which would have made the back-panel small enough to wear fitting the waist line while giving enough fabric to wear over the bustle. The waistband is one inch in width. A six-inch opening on the right side of the skirt reveals a pocket made of white chintz.

The inside of the hem edge shows a seven-inch deep hem facing. The hem edge is protected with grosgrain ribbon. The hem decoration consists of a seven inch ruffle on which there are two rows of two-inch-wide ruching. Two rows of delicate hand stitching forms each row of ruching, this forming a puff effect in the ruffle.

The only dress trim that remains is a large, bright coral silk bow with twenty-five-inch-long sashes. The ribbon used to make the bow is two and a half inches wide. The bow itself is ten inches in width and has four layers of ties. The knot keeping it intact is one and a half inches deep and one and three-fourths inches in width. The bow was removed from the dress. Most likely it was worn on the back of the bodice at the waistline. It would have draped over the skirt's bustle. (Location: ALPL, Springfield, Illinois.)

Coral Necklace
1871

While it is not known for sure, it is believed that this coral necklace was worn with the white and coral dress at St. James Court. Family history has maintained that Mary wore coral jewelry to match her gown. This necklace is the exact shade of coral as the ribbon that graced her dress. Other pieces of Mary's coral jewelry have a lighter hue.

There are twenty-nine beads on the left and thirty beads on the right of the necklace. It closes with a barrel clasp.

As the necklace would rest on the collarbone, each side has a bouquet of leaves and roses with a small angel's face on top of each bouquet. These two bouquets are brought together by a single coral rose.

The large medallion, which hangs from the single coral rose, is a two-inch detachable brooch mounted on a simple gold wire with a simple clasp. A cherub surrounded by a flowing ribbon and holding a wreath of roses sits on top of a large bouquet of roses and leaves.

This necklace would not normally be considered mourning jewelry because of its vivid coral hue. However, the design of the piece contains symbols commonly used in mourning jewelry. The cherub's wreath of roses represents never-ending love — such as that of a spouse. Roses were quite common in mourning jewelry. Angels or cherubs were often used to represent children who had passed away. If Mary did indeed wear this to St. James Court, the two small cherub heads may have represented Eddie and Willie while the larger cherub holding the wreath may have represented Abraham. Robert and Tad were both living at the time this necklace was worn. (Location: ALPL, Springfield, Illinois.)

Coral Necklace, 1871. (Photograph by Jim Helm courtesy of Abraham Lincoln
Presidential Library & Museum (ALPLM) Springfield, IL)

Black Dress, Deep Mourning Circa 1872

By this time, most women had replaced their bonnets with hats. Older women and many widows continued to wear a bonnet which was worn higher on the forehead. Mary's seems to be tilted for artistic purposes.

What is most noticeable about Mary's costume is the blackness and plainness of the design. Her bonnet strings are black. A black shawl covers the bodice of the dress. Her cuffs and collar are black. She wears no visible jewelry; even her wedding ring is hidden from the view of the camera's lens. It is possible that she is not wearing it. Family members often recalled that her hands became swollen and she could no longer wear her wedding ring. Her hands do appear swollen in the photograph, and it is possible that Mary deliberately covered her left hand to hide a missing ring.

Although Mary's dress is not visible due to her shawl, it would have followed the basic style of the 1870s. By this time, the crinoline was gone. Women's skirts contained a bustle. These were made either by a steel frame as the crinoline had been, or they were made by stiff horsehair ruffles.[238] The massive amount of fabric in the skirt was gathered and placed over the bustle. The polonaise bodice was the most popular fashion. Often it was described as "being in the Pompadour style with square opening in front, sleeves tight to the elbow and finished with open frills.[239] Of course, a widow would forgo the frills.

When Tad, the youngest Lincoln son, died in 1871, Mary was left alone. She always had a strong belief in spiritualism which helped satisfy her desires to reach those who were lost to her. When Mary attended a séance in Boston, she believed she felt Lincoln's hands rest on her shoulders. Spirit photographer William H. Mumler reinforced her belief when he presented her with this photograph as "proof" that Lincoln's spirit did indeed visit and comfort her.[240] Mary may have been convinced, but son Robert was not. This provided one more piece of evidence for him to doubt his mother's ability to reason and make rational choices.

Black Dress, Deep Mourning, Circa 1872. (Photograph courtesy of The Lincoln Museum, Fort Wayne, IN (Reference #109) [identified as ML, O-26])

Black Mourning Bodice
Circa 1881

In 1875, Robert brought his mother to trial on charges of insanity. At a time in history when women had few legal rights and limited social position, the closest living male was considered responsible for an unmarried woman. Robert accepted these responsibilities and kept a watchful eye on his mother's ever increasing spending. He went as far as to hire a Pinkerton detective to follow her and report her whereabouts and purchases. Mary continued to purchase jewelry, household goods, and other items which she tended to place in her trunks.

Robert believed Mary's behavior to be an indication of lunacy; he consulted six doctors who agreed. Under legal advisement from Leonard Swett, Robert wrote to the involved physicians "asking them for their written opinions of Mrs. Lincoln's condition."[241] A petition for trial was filed early in the day on May 19, 1875. When Mary was brought to the court room later that same day, she found the judge, jury, witnesses, and even her lawyer were there at Robert's request. She said nothing during the three hours she listened to seventeen witnesses described her shopping habits, mood, and somewhat eccentric behavior. No one, not even her attorney, said anything in her defense. A jury of twelve men agreed with Robert and declared, "Mary Lincoln is insane and is a fit person to be sent to a State Hospital for the Insane."[242]

The next day Robert was appointed conservator of his mother's estate, and Mary was placed in a private sanitarium called Bellevue Place in Batavia, Illinois. There she was treated by Dr. Patterson who believed the best treatment was "rest, diet, baths, fresh air, occupation, diversion, change of scene, and no more medicine than necessary."[243] At Bellevue, Mary lived in a small room, often took her meals with the Patterson family, took walks about the grounds, and occasionally enjoyed a carriage

Black Mourning Bodice, Circa 1881. (Photograph author's collection)

ride. She lived a rather solitary life; "her sole contact with the community seemed to be through association with a local dressmaker."[244]

She also made plans to regain her freedom. In a series of letters Mary was able to contact Judge James B. Bradwell and his wife Myra, who also was an attorney. A campaign to free Mary Lincoln began. They spoke to reporters, Dr. Patterson, and Robert about Mary's release, and on September 10, 1875, she was allowed to go and live with her sister Elizabeth Edwards. Her total time at Bellevue had been less than four months.

Mary continued to shop. Just two months after she moved to Springfield, Robert complained to Judge David Davis that his mother had purchased yet another new bonnet.

On June 15, 1876, a second trial was held. Leonard Swett, the man who had worked to commit Mary a year before, was the attorney hired in her defense. Mary only had one witness, her brother-in-law Ninian Edwards. This time, Robert said nothing. A jury quickly attached their signatures to the verdict and announced, "Mary Lincoln is restored to reason and is capable to manage and control her estate."[245]

Mary continued to live with Ninian and Elizabeth for a few months, and then traveled once more to Europe. She mostly stayed in Pau, France. There she lived a quiet life until she fell and injured her back in 1880. She then returned to Springfield where she could rest and be among family in her sister's home.

But for Mary there was no true rest. She suffered from "chronic inflammation of the spinal cord, chronic disease of the kidneys, and commencing cataract of both eyes."[246] Light hurt her eyes, pain shot through her body, and she suffered from feeling hot. In 1881 she traveled to New York City for "treatment for a disease of the eyes and for diabetes."[247] Her last photograph shows that her hands and face were swollen. In October 1879 Mary wrote to her nephew, "My great bloat has left me & I have returned to my natural size." In another letter, Mary wrote, "Tell your dear Grandma, I have now run down to 100-pounds, EXACTLY."[248]

This was Mary's physical condition when she wore this black mourning bodice.

A pleated, stand-up collar is attached to the bodice. One row of piping is between the collar and the bodice neckline. All other seams on the bodice have double piping. Tight-fitted sleeves end with a four-inch-deep cuff that closes at the wrist with three buttons.

The tight-fitted bodice is approximately twenty-eight inches in length. With a hemline this far below the waistline, the garment gave the wearer the popular stiff figure. The bodice is void of all trims and decorations except for a four-inch-deep ruffle along the bottom edge of the bodice. Twenty half-inch black covered buttons create the bodice's front closure.

The small, round mourning bonnet has a knot holding the seven folds of fabric in place. The bonnet, bodice, and fan were given to Mary's sister, Frances Wallace.

The skirt to this costume has not been preserved. From fashion plates of the era, a hobble skirt was appropriate. These skirts received their name because they were straight, tight, sheath skirts, and wearing one made the wearer "hobble" when she walked, without being able to take a stride of natural length. Fashionable skirts were heavily trimmed. The most fashionable women wore skirts that had a horizontal trim or drapery trim. Bodice sleeves were "long, plain, and tight" and the most fashionable bodice no longer laced up the back, but "fastened with a row of buttons down the front."[249] With a plain bodice and a decorated skirt, the fashionable lady's overall appearance was "plain above, fancy below."[250]

Mary's bodice shows that even in her last years, and as a widow mourning her husband seventeen years after his death, she still maintained her fashionable appearance. (Location: Mary Todd Lincoln House, Lexington, Kentucky.)

White Silk Burial Dress
July 16, 1882

During the last years of Mary's life, her health prevented her from doing many things. She mostly stayed in her room at Elizabeth's and lived within her memories. All of Mary's possessions were placed in trunks and stored in Elizabeth's home

In a letter to their half-sister, Emily Todd Helm, Ann wrote about their older sister Mary and her trunks:

> Mrs. Lincoln stays in her room mends her dresses and unpacks her trunks 36 in number and wants to be considered an invalid and Bob likes it as she is not making purchases. The last this winter is a silk cloak lined with white ermine $400 and a lace shawl totaling $700. Poor thing, falling greatness and partial decay of intellect is a hard thing to contend against.[251]

Another relative, Mary Brown, the granddaughter of Elizabeth Edwards, recalled that one of the floors sagged from the weight of sixty-four trunks and crates which were packed with "a lot of clothes." Miss Brown continued, "Every day she got up and went through those trunks for hours. Grandmother said it was funny, if Aunt Mary was so sick, that she was able to be up all day bending over her trunks."[252]

Mary spent most of her time looking at her treasurer and remembering happier times. She also was preoccupied with a deep desire to die and was convinced she would do so soon. Her letters were filled with comments about a blissful death, of how she longed to be reunited with her loved and lost, and how she wished she had been slain along with her husband. In a letter written to Dr. Willis Danforth, Mary outlined her desired funeral arrangements:

> I wish my remains to be clothed in the white silk dress — which will be found in the lower drawer of the bureau in my room.

I desire that my body shall remain for two days (48) hours, without the lid of the coffin being screwed down. . . . My coffin I wish to be of solid rosewood plain, but massive silver plate with this inscription " 'Mary Lincoln' Died __ __ ____ He giveth his beloved sleep.' " On the fourth 4th day after my decease, I wish my remains placed beside my dear husband & Taddie's on one side of me.[253]

On the afternoon of July 15, 1882, Mary collapsed. The Edwards' family doctor, T. W. Dresser, came and pronounced that there was nothing he could do. The next evening, July 16, at 8:15, Mary received her "beloved sleep."

It is not known if Mary wore the white dress she mentioned in her letter to Dr. Danforth. It is believed she was buried in a white dress, for after her death Elizabeth and Ninian sent a telegram to Chicago for white silk.[254] Often, white was considered the deepest mourning color, and people were given "white funerals."

Mary's body lay in the north double parlor of the Edwards' home, the same parlor in which she had married Abraham some forty years before. The newspaper reporters remarked that her "hands were visible in the casket" and they "noticed her wedding ring."[255]

The funeral service was held at the First Presbyterian Church on July 19. Springfield businesses closed in honor of Mary, and the church was filled with mourners. In the front row sat Mary's only surviving son, Robert, and her sister Frances Wallace, who was heavily veiled and mourning her own husband. Pallbearers included Governor Shelby Cullom, Judge Samuel H. Treat (judge of the United States District Court), Esq. James Conklin (friend to Lincoln and Mary since prior to their marriage), John Williams (a Springfield merchant and banker), John S. Bradford, and Jacob Bunn (both Springfield merchants), and a few other prominent men of the city.

The church was decorated with several large floral displays. A three-foot-tall floral representation of "Pearly Gates Ajar" stood behind Mary's casket. Under this symbolic arch was a bust of Abraham Lincoln. A

Engraving of Mary Lincoln's Funeral. (Engraving by unknown artist, courtesy Abraham Lincoln Presidential Library & Museum [ALPLM], Springfield, IL)

five-foot-tall floral cross and a floral pillow were memorials from the "Citizens of Springfield." A large book crafted from carnations had "Mary Lincoln" written in forget-me-nots. A broken column with a representation of a white dove perched on its top stood at the foot of the casket.[256] The altar was festooned with black crape.

Three ministers spoke at the funeral. Reverend R. O. Post of the First Congregation Church read from the Bible and led a prayer. Reverend James A. Reed from First Presbyterian Church gave the sermon in which he compared Abraham and Mary Lincoln's lives to two large pine trees which had grown so closely together that their roots were intertwined. One was killed during a storm, and within a few years, the remaining tree wasted away and died as well — and so it was with Abraham and Mary. The funeral ended with a prayer by Reverend T. A. Parker of First Methodist Church.[257]

The mourners followed the carriage hearse to Oak Ridge Cemetery where Mary's body was placed in a crypt beside her husband.[258]

Mary had once written to Senator Charles Sumner:

My belief, is so assured that Death, is only a blessed transition to the "pure in heart," that a very slight veil separates us, from the "loved & lost" and to me, there is comfort, in the thought, that though unseen by us, they are very near.[259]

For Mary, the veil had been lifted, and she at long last had her blessed reunion with her "loved & lost."

Epilogue

What became of Mary's trunks which were filled with her clothing, treasures, and mementoes of her life? For a while they remained at the home of Elizabeth Edwards. Mary, like Abraham, died without a will, leaving Robert her sole heir. The task of sorting through the trunks and dividing their contents fell upon Robert and his wife, Mary Harlan Lincoln.

Many of Mary's belongings remained in Springfield and were given to members of the Todd family. One of Mary's bonnets, a cravat, a china ink well, photographs, the famous point lace bertha, and the watch Lincoln carried the night of his assassination were given to Emily Todd Helm and her children. Jewelry was also given to the daughters of Elizabeth Edwards, Frances Wallace, and Levi Todd.

The bulk of the trunks were sent to the Lincolns' home in Mount Pleasant, Iowa, the home of Mary Harlan Lincoln's childhood. After the death of her parents, Mary and Robert owned the home and used it as a summer residence. Their children attended school there and developed friendships within the community. It was there that Robert and Mary finished the task of sorting through the trunks.

Some of the things were of historical value and needed to be preserved for museums and archives. Robert sorted through all of his father's documents, destroying personal papers and donating the rest to the Library of Congress. Some items were kept for family use. Family portraits hung on the walls of Robert's home, and some of the silver pieces that had once been used in the White House were now used by Robert's family.

Robert and Mary had two daughters of their own, Mary and Jessie. They enjoyed playing with their grandmother's old dresses and admired the richness of the fabric and laces. It was also their joy to share a piece of Lincoln history with their friends. They would cut Mary's gowns apart and use the fabric to make reticules for their friends. One of these small

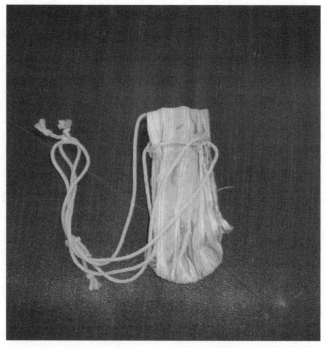
Reticule. (Photograph courtesy of the Harlan-Lincoln House Collection at Iowa Wesleyan College, Mt. Pleasant, Iowa)

purses has survived and is now owned by the Harlan-Lincoln House. It is likely the two girls made other items for their friends as well. To them, the dresses were not important historical artifacts, but nothing more than old clothes. The embarrassment Robert had suffered from the Old Clothes Scandal probably left him with the belief that old clothing would never have any historical significance. Thus he most likely would not have refused his daughters in their quest of giving gifts to friends.

Some of Mary's dresses given as gifts were altered to fit the receiver. After all, why own a dress made of exquisite, rich, French fabric if it does not fit? It is not known if the Lincoln granddaughters altered any of their grandmother's dresses to wear themselves, though it is known from photographs that, like their grandmother, they were fashionable women. They inherited their grandmother's sense of fashion and love of fine clothing.

Glossary

Alazarin: A form of red.

Basque: A skirt-like extension on the back of a bodice. A bodice often had more than one basque of varying lengths.

Basque bodice: A bodice with one or more basques attached. This type of bodice is also commonly referred to as a basque.

Bertha: A caplet attached to the neckline of an evening gown. A bertha was made on a casing with a drawstring and could be worn with more than one garment.

Boucle: A woven or knitted fabric with a drawn-out, ringed, or looped yarn to give it a kinky appearance at intervals. Made in a variety of weights, the fabric is usually springy to handle.

Cache-peigne: Something worn in the hair to hide a comb.

Cincture: A belt.

Corsage: The front of an evening bodice.

Décolletage: The neckline of an evening bodice.

Drab: A brownish-gray color.

Epaulette: Most often an ornamental shoulder piece on dress and full-dress military uniforms; however, in a lady's wardrobe it can be made in military style, or it can be a decorative strip or loop of fabric on the shoulder of a coat or dress.

Fanchon: A white, triangular shaped, day cap worn indoors. After 1864, the Fanchon bonnet was popular.

Fluting: Any groove or furrow as in a ruffle of cloth.

Havannah: A color in the brown family that was between a cinnamon and an olive brown.

In Absentia: To be present at an event, but to abstain for the social activities association with the event.

Jockey: A flat piece of fabric used as trim and sewn into the shoulder seams, which covers the outer part of the shoulder and hides the seam. The lower edge of the jockey was left free and was often trimmed with ribbon or lace.

Levee: a formal reception to honor someone.

Mantle: A loose, cape like garment.

Merino: A thin woolen twilled cloth made from the wool of Spanish Merino sheep.

Nail: A measurement used in garment construction. One nail is the equivalent of two and a half inches.

Sacque and Petticoat: A two-piece costume consisting of a loose fitting bodice with loose sleeves and a plain skirt. The petticoat can be lopped up for outdoor activities. This style of garment was often worn in rural settings.

Tablier (en tablier): A skirt with a contrasting design or fabric down the front, emulating an apron-like appearance. In the 1840s these were often trimmed with lace inserts or ribbons. In the 1860s it was fashionable to quilt the tablier.

Parure: Ornaments or jewels.

Peplum: A short flounce, attached to or extending from the waistline of a snugly fitting bodice, jacket, or dress.

Passementerie: Braid, trimmings.

Postillions: A long basque with a center split thus making two "posts" of fabric.

Portmonnaie: A wallet, coin purse, or something to carry money.

Quilling: A pleated trim.

Ruching: A narrow trim gathered along a thread sewn in the center of the strip. Each edge was finished.

Wrapper: A loose-fitting robe intended to be worn at home. Often women on the frontier used them as their day dresses.

Acknowledgments

My interest in Mary Lincoln's wardrobe began on a family vacation when I was a young child. We traveled to Gatlinburg, Tennessee, and explored the contents of the American History Wax Museum. I was enthralled with the wax figures and dioramas that seemed so lifelike. A couple of scenes fascinated me more than others, but it was the scene of the Lincoln Assassination that began my interest in Mary Lincoln. The depiction was simple. Mary sat in a chair with her husband in a rocker beside her; John Wilkes Booth stood behind Lincoln, his derringer aimed at the President's head. I was mesmerized by the simplicity of it all, and wondered if that was indeed the type of dress Mary wore that night. I have since learned that it was not.

My quest for details about Mary Lincoln and the clothes she wore had begun. It has been a long journey to this book, and many individuals and institutions have my heartfelt gratitude for their role in helping me along the way.

Libraries and Museums

One of the most enjoyable adventures when researching this project was going to the depositories were some of Mary's actual garments are located. The staffs, directors, and curators at these libraries and museums were a tremendous help. The Abraham Lincoln Presidential Library in Museum gave me the opportunity to see the black silk dress with embroidered berries. When gazing at it, one has to wonder how many hours were needed to create such an exquisite piece of art. It is a prime example of the luxurious fabrics and lace which were part of Mary's wardrobe. My sincerest thanks go to Mr. Kim Bauer, the curator of the Lincoln Collection at the time of my research trips for allowing me to study Mary's wardrobe. Jane Ehrenhart, Jan Perone, and Dr. Tom Schwartz were wonderful help in pointing me in the right direction for tidbits of information and helping me find much needed sources. Thanks also go to Jennifer Ericson and Jim Helm for getting all of the photographs together.

Thanks go to Bryan McDaniel at the Chicago History Museum for obtaining some very elusive photographs. Former staff members at the Chicago History Museum were instrumental in providing detailed construction materials about the garments in their collection.

Clark Evans at the Library of Congress provided valuable information about Mrs. Lincoln's Tiffany seed-pearl parure.

Cindy Van Horn at The Lincoln Museum Research Library in Fort Wayne, Indiana, was invaluable during the process of this project. Her knowledge of the collection at the library and her timely response to my requests are much appreciated.

Thanks go to Gwen Thompson, director of the Mary Todd Lincoln House in Lexington, Kentucky, for allowing the black bodice to be photographed.

Michelle Gullion and her staff at the National First Ladies Library and Museum were a tremendous help by acquiring photographs and providing information about the dresses in their collection.

Lisa Kathleen Graddy at the Smithsonian was extremely helpful by providing detailed information about the royal purple dress in the Divisions of Political History.

Individuals

Even though he is also listed as a staff member of the ALPLM, Kim Bauer deserves extra acknowledgment for his continued support and encouragement to complete this task, even after he began a new position.

For years, Donna Daniels has encouraged me to write this manuscript. She is one of the people I go to whenever I need a Lincoln book that is not in my own library. She was also one of the people who read and critiqued a few passages. Thanks to her and her husband, Max, for all of their research help and words of encouragement throughout this project.

Another one whose library I often check is Valerie Gugala. Thanks to her for helping find much-needed newspaper articles and for all our discussions about Mary's wardrobe.

While looking at photos of Mary, I realized that I know very little about flowers. Thanks to Martha Henderson for her keen eye and for helping identify some of the flowers in Mary's headdresses and floral sprays. Also, Edward Norton for use of his photograph of Mary and for providing valuable information about the Tiffany seed-pearl parure. And to Terry Esvelt for providing Todd family information and a little-known dress description that had been passed through the family.

My deepest and sincerest thanks go to those who read and reread the manuscript: Gerald Swick and Greta Ratliff. Gerald offered writing advice, historical information, and lots of fabulous discussion about Mary Lincoln in general. Greta served as a fashion editor and French teacher; she made sure the historical fashion terms were correct, the French spelling and vocabulary were correct, and the costume descriptions were vivid.

And finally, thank you to my editor, Sheila Samson, who knows how to take a plain manuscript and transform it into a beautiful work of art.

Endnotes

i. Turner, Justn & Linda Levitt Turner, *Mary Todd Lincoln, Her Life and Letters*, p. 20.

ii. Gernsheim, Alison, *Victorian and Edwardian Fashion, A Photographic Survey*, p. 26.

iii. Neely, Mark E. Jr. and R. Gerald McMurtry, *The Insanity File: The Case of Mary Todd Lincoln*, p. 154.

iv. Ibid., p. 174.

v. Often seen referred to as *Godey's Ladies' Magazine*, this publication was founded by Louis A. Godey in 1830. Seven years later, in 1837, Godey purchased *The Ladie's Magazine*, which was edited by Sarah Josepha Hale. His main reason for purchasing this second publication was to hire Mrs. Hale, who served as editor for *Godey's* from 1837 until 1878.

1. Cunnington, C. Willett, *English Women's Clothing in the Nineteenth Century*, p. 95.

2. Letter, From Elizabeth Humphreys Norris to Emily Todd Helm, September 28, 1895. Manuscript Department, SC1980, ALPL

3. Ibid.

4. Ibid.

5. Ibid.

6. Helm, Katherine, *Mary, Wife of Lincoln*, pp. 29–30.

7. *Lincoln's Marriage, Newspaper Interview with Mrs. Frances Wallace, Springfield, IL September 2, 1895*, Lincoln Collection, ALPL

8. Helm, K., p. 34.

9. Ibid., p. 33.

10. Kunhardt, Philip B. Jr., Philip B. Kunhardt III, Peter W. Kunhardt, *Lincoln: An Illustrated Biography*, p. 56.

11. Helm, K., p. 74.

12. Ibid.

13. Ibid., p. 86.

14. Ibid., p. 82.

15. Gordon, Beulah. "Coffee Spilled on Borrowed Nuptial Gown of Mary Todd," *Illinois State Journal,* August 16, 1942, The Lincoln Museum, Fort Wayne, IN.

16. Randall, Ruth Painter, *Mary Lincoln, Biography of a Marriage,* p. 72.

17. *Lincoln's Marriage, Newspaper Interview with Mrs. Frances Wallace, Springfield, IL September 2, 1895,* Lincoln Collection, ALPL

18. Ibid.

19. Helm, K., p. 95

20. *Lincoln's Marriage.*

21. Ostendorf, Lloyd, *The Photographs of Mary Todd Lincoln.*

22. Ostendorf, p. 274.

23. Cunnington, p. 146.

24. Ibid., p. 143.

25. Stuart, Emily Huntington, *Some Recollections of the Early Days in Springfield and Remeniscences of Abraham Lincoln and Other Celebrities who Lived in that Little Town in My Youth,* p. 1086.

26. Gernsheim, Alison, p. 27.

27. Helm, K., p. 106.

28. Ibid.

29. Ibid.

30. Cunnington, p. 178.

31. Ibid., p. 177.

32. Ibid., p. 177.

33. Ibid., p. 178.

34. Ibid., p. 185.

35. Ibid.

36. Helm, K., p. 109.

37. Ibid.

38. Cunnington, p. 185.

39. Gernsheim, Alison, p. 44.

40. Randall, Ruth Painter, pp. 151–152.

41. Hale, Sarah Josepha, *Early American Cookery, "The Good Housekeeper,"* *1841*, p. 135.

42. Cunnington, p. 189.

43. Olian, Jo Anne, *80 Godey's Full-Color Fashion Plates 1838-1880*, p. 5.

44. Gersheim, p. 47.

45. Randall, p. 191.

46. Helm, K., p. 153.

47. James, Jeannie H. and Wayne C. Temple, "Mrs. Lincoln's Clothing," *Lincoln Herald,* Summer, 1960, p. 57.

48. Helm, K., pp. 155-156.

49. Ibid., p. 162

50. Searcher, Victor, *Lincoln's Journey to Greatness*, p. 42.

51. Ibid., p. 72.

52. Ibid., p. 150.

53. Ibid., p. 210.

54. Durbin, Louise, *Inaugural Cavalcade*, p. 80.

55. Miers, Earl Schenck, Editor-in-Chief, *Lincoln Day by Day: A Chronology 1809 – 1865*, p. 10.

56. Grimsley, Elizabeth Todd, "Six Months in the White House," *Journal of the Illinois State Historical Society*, Vol. XIX, October, 1926–January, 1927 Nos. 3–4, p. 45.

57. Durbin, Louise, p. 86.

58. *Frank Leslie's Illustrated Newspaper,* March 23, 1861, p. 285, column 1.

59. Kunhardt et al, p. 147.

60. Ibid.

61. *The New York Times,* March 6, 1861, ALPL.

62. Ibid.

63. Kinnaid, Virginia, *Mrs. Lincoln as a White House Hostess*, pp. 6–7.

64. *The New York Times*, March 6, 1861. ALPL

65. Fales, Martha Gandy, *Jewelry in America: 1600–1900*, p. 211.

66. Holzer, Harold, Press Release for The Metropolitan Museum of Art, New York, NY, May 22, 2000 and Loring John, *Tiffany's 150 Years*, p. 47.

67. Fales, Martha Gandy, p. 211.

68. Ibid., p. 213.

69. Keckley, Elizabeth, *Behind the Scenes*, p. 79.

70. Ibid., p. 86.

71. Ibid., p. 90.

72. Ibid., p. 88.

73. Gersheim, p. 45.

74. Cunnington, p. 208.

75. *New York Herald*, March 13, 1861

76. Miers, section 1861–1865, p. 28.

77. Bayne, Julia Taft, *Tad Lincoln's Father*, p. 3.

78. Ibid., pp. 18–20.

79. Swisshell, Jane Grey, "Tribute to the Dead," *Chicago Tribune,* July 20, 1882, p. 7.

80. Ostendorf, p. 292.

81. Keckley, p. 101.

82. Gernsheim, p. 49.

83. Cunnington, p. 214.

84. *Lexington* (Kentucky) *Observer and Reporter*, February 15, 1862.

85. Ostendorf, p. 298.

86. Shep, R. L., *Civil War Ladies: Fashions and Needle-Arts of the Early 1860s*, p. 38.

87. Cunnington, p. 210.

88. Ostendorf, p. 314.

89. Smithsonian Institution, National Museum of American History, Division of Politics & Reform, First Ladies Collection, Catalog file #241232.1

90. Ibid.

91. Helm, K., p. 177.

92. Randall, p. 221.

93. Cunnington, p. 244.

94. James and Temple, p. 60.

95. Gernsheim, p. 31.

96. Kunhardt et al, p. 276.

97. Turner, p. 88.

98. Grimsley, p. 58.

99. James and Temple, p. 60.

100. Bayne, p. 70.

101. James and Temple, p. 60.

102. Helm, K., p. 177.

103. Turner, p. 283.

104. Ostendorf, p. 282.

105. Cunnington, p. 210.

106. Ibid., p. 208.

107. Ostendorf, p. 284.

108. *Frank Leslie's Illustrated Newspaper,* February 22, 1862, p. 209, column 1.

109. Miers, Earl Schenck, section 1861–1865, p. 83; Temple, p. 61.

110. Bayne, p. 71.

111. Smithsonian Institution, National Museum of American History, Division of Politics & Reform, First Ladies' Collection, Catalog card #33280B.

112. Smithsonian Institution, National Museum of American History, Division of Politics & Reform, First Ladies' Collection, Catalog card #33280D.

113. "New Year's Day Reception at the White House," *Chicago Tribune,* January 9, 1864, pp. 0–2.

114. Miers, Earl Schenck, section 1861–1865, p. 87.

115. *Chicago Tribune,* January 6, 1862, p. 1.

116. *Harper's Weekly,* January 25, 1862. Singleton, Esther, *The Story of the White House.*

117. Cunnington, p. 208.

118. Randall, pp. 222–223.

119. Miers, section 1861–1865, p. 90; Temple p. 61.

120. Bayne, p. 71.

121. "The Levee at the White House," *Chicago Tribune,* January 29, 1862, pp. 0–3.

122. *Harper's Weekly* newspaper, November 8, 1862, p. 700, column 1.

123. Cunnington, p. 211.

124. *Frank Leslie's Illustrated Newspaper*, February 22, 1862, p. 209, column 1.

125. Miers, section 1861–1865, p. 95.

126. *Frank Leslie's Illustrated Newspaper*, February 22, 1862, p. 213, columns 2 and 3.

127. Ibid., p. 214.

128. Keckley, p. 101.

129. Miers, section 1861–1865, p. 93.

130. Green, Harvey, and Mary Ellen Perry, *The Light of the Home: An Intimate View of the Lives of Women in Victorian America*, p. 167.

131. Mehaffey, Karen Rae, *The After-Life: Mourning Rituals and The Mid-Victorians.*

132. Ibid.

133. Majka, Holly, *Life in the Midst of Death: A Victorian Manual for Mourning*, pp. 39–40.

134. Green, Harvey and Mary Ellen Perry, p. 170.

135. Mehaffey, Karen Rae, *The After-Life: Mourning Rituals and The Mid-Victorians,* Laser Writers Publishing, Pipestone, MN, c. 1993.

136. Ibid.

137. Ibid.

138. Kunhardt et al, p, 174.

139. Letter, Elizabeth Edwards to Julia Edwards Baker, March 2, 1862, Manuscript Department, SC 445, ALPLM, Springfield, IL.

140. Ibid.

141. Randall, p. 297.

142. Meirs, section 1861–1865, p. 102.

143. Ibid., p. 104.

144. Randall, p. 296.

145. Ibid., p. 342.

146. James and Temple, p. 61.

147. Randall, p. 320.

148. Ibid.

149. Randall, p. 320; and Meirs, section 1861–1865, p. 168.

150. Randall, p. 320.

151. Kunhardt et al, p. 205.

152. Nicolay, Helen, *Lincoln's Secretary: A Biography of John G. Nicolay*, p. 167.

153. Cunnington, p. 213.

154. Ibid., p. 214.

155. Ostendorf, p. 288.

156. Cunnington, p. 244.

157. Ibid., p. 216.

158. "Mrs. Lincoln at Mount Washington," *Chicago Tribune,* August 14, 1863, p. 2.

159. Ibid.

160. Cunnington, p. 190.

161. Blum, Stella, *Fashions and Costumes from Godey's Lady's Book,* p. 54.

162. Helm, K., p. 217.

163. Helm, Emily Todd, Random notes from her war-time diary, Mary Townsend Murphy Collection, private.

164. Ibid.

165. Ibid.

166. *Chicago Tribune,* December 30, 1863, p. 3.

167. Gernsheim, p. 29.

168. Keckley, p. 348.

169. "New Year's Reception at the White House, *Chicago Tribune,* January 9, 1864, pp. 0–2.

170. Ibid.

171. Burlingame, Michael, *Lincoln Observed: Civil War Dispatches of Noah Brooks,* John Hopkins University Press, c. 1998, p. 100.

172. James and Temple, p. 62.

173. Ostendorf, p. 323; and Charles Hamilton and Lloyd Ostendorf, *Lincoln in Photographs: An Album of Every Known Pose,* p. 298.

174. Cunnington, p. 245.

175 *The Collective Works of Abraham Lincoln,* entry for October 3, 1863, Volume 6, pp. 496–497. 176. Kunhardt, p. 220; and Harold Holzer, Gabor S. Boritt, and Mark E. Neely Jr., p. 160.

177. Cunnington, p. 216.

178. Ostendorf, p. 320.

179. Cunnington, p. 219.

180. Ibid., p. 220.

181. Ibid. p. 222.

182. Holzer, Harold, Gabor S. Boritt, Mark E. Neely Jr., *The Lincoln Image: Abraham Lincoln and the Popular Print*, p. 175.

183. Ibid.

184. Meirs, Earl Schenck, section 1861–1865, p. 305.

185. Randall, p. 366.

186. Gernsheim, p. 48.

187. Meirs, section 1861–1865, p. 306.

188. Randall, p. 366.

189. James and Temple, p. 63.

190. Cunnington, p. 222.

191. Meirs, section 1861–1865, p. 306.

192. Helm, K., p. 228.

193. Randall, p. 367.

194. *Washington Chronicle,* January 22, 1865.

195. Blum, Stella, p. 64; Olian, JoAnne, page Plate 29.

196. Kinnaid, Virginia, p. 15.

197. Durbin, Louisa, p. 89.

198. James and Temple, p. 63.

199. Durbin, Louisa pp. 89–90.

200. Ibid.

201. *New York Times,* March 7, 1865. ALPL

202. Ibid., March 8, 1865. ALPL

203. Baker, Jean, *Mary Todd Lincoln: A Biography*, W. W. Norton & Co., New York, c. 1987, p. 237.

204. Turner, pp. 270–271.

205. Meirs, section 1861–1865, p. 329.

206. Turner, pp. 284–285.

207. Randall, p. 382.

208. Ibid.

209. Kunhardt, Dorothy Meserve and Philip B. Kunhardt Jr., *Twenty Days: A Narrative in Text and Pictures of the Assassination of Abraham Lincoln and the Twenty Days and Nights that followed — The Nation in Mourning, the Long Trip Home to Springfield,* Castle Books, Secaucus, NJ, c. 1965 & 1993, p. 79.

210. Randall, p. 384.

211. Kunhardt, Dorothy Meserve and Philip B. Kunhardt, Jr., p. 80.

212. Holzer, Harold, Gabor S. Boritt, and Mary E. Neely Jr., p. 153.

213. Kunhardt, Dorothy Meserve and Philip B. Kunhardt J., pp. 100–101.

214. Keckley, p. 202.

215. Tuner, p. 240.

216. Ibid., p. 244.

217. Ibid., p. 466.

218. Ibid., p. 441.

219. Cunnington, p. 227.

220. Keckley, pp. 269–270.

221. "Disgraceful," *The Conservative ,*Clarksburg, WV, November 9, 1867

222. Randall, p. 412.

223. Ibid., p. 413.

224. Keckley, p. 332.

225. Ibid., pp. 347–348.

226. "Mrs. Lincoln," *Wheeling Intelligencer,* Thursday, October 10, 1867, p. 1, column 2.

227. "Mrs. Lincoln and her Wardrobe," *Chicago Tribune*, October 7, 1867, front page, column 2.

228. Ibid & *Wheeling Intelligencer*, October 10, 1867.

229. Keckley, pp. 327–328.

230. Ibid., p. 365.

231. Ibid., p. 14

232. Randall, p. 414.

233. James and Temple, p. 64.

234. Randall, page 421.

235. Swisshelm, Jane Grey, "Tribute to the Dead," *Chicago Tribune*, July 20, 1882, page 7.

236. This scenario seems to have first appeared in the play *The Last of Mrs. Lincoln*.

237. *The State Journal-Register*, May 3, 1976, p. 21.

238. Olian, Jo Anne, p. 5.

239. Cunnington, p. 262.

240. Kunhardt et al, p. 397.

241. Ross, Rodney A., "Mary Todd Lincoln, Patient At Bellevue Place, Batavia," *Journal of the Illinois State Historical Society*, Spring 1970, p. 7.

242. Verdict of the Jury, May 19, 1875, Chicago Historical Society, Lincoln Collection, 1876, Box 236, Folder 306.

243. Ross, Rodney, A., p. 10.

244. Ibid., p. 11.

245. Ibid., p. 22.

246. Hirschhorn, Norbert and Robert G. Feldman, "Mary Lincoln's Final Illness: A Medical and Historical Reappraisal," *Journal of the History of Medicine*, Vol. 54, October 1999, p. 518.

247. Ibid., p. 536.

248. Turner, pp. 600, 693.

249. Gernshein, p. 68.

250. Ibid.

251. Smith, Ann, to Emily Todd Helm, Letter, June 19 (no year, but believed to be 1881), private collection.

252. Kunhardt et al, pp. 396–397.

253. Letter, From Mary Lincoln to Dr. Willis Danforth, August 1874, ALPLM.

254. Neely and McMurtry, p. 123.

255. "Mary Todd Lincoln (1818–1882), *Lincoln Lore,* Bulletin of the Lincoln Library and Museum, Edited by Mark Neely, Jr., November 1981, Number 1725, p. 1.

256. Ibid., p. 2.

257. Ibid.

258. "Mrs. Abraham Lincoln," *Chicago Tribune,* July 20, 1882, p. 3, column 2. NOTE: The current burial positions were not arranged until after an attempt to steal Lincoln's body had occurred.

259. Turner, p. 256.

Bibliography

Books

Baker, Jean. *Mary Todd Lincoln: A Biography.* New York: W. W. Norton & Co., c. 1987.

Basler, Roy P., Editor, Assistant Editors, Marion Dobress Pratt, Lloyd A. Dunlap. *The Collective Works of Abraham Lincoln.* Entry for October 3, 1863, Volume 6. Rutgers University Press, c. 1953.

Bayne, Julia Taft. *Tad Lincoln's Father.* Lincoln, NB: University of Nebraska Press, c. 2001.

Blum, Stella. *Fashions and Costumes from Godey's Lady's Book.* New York: Dover Publications, Inc., c. 1985.

Burlingame, Michael. *Lincoln Observed: Civil War Dispatches of Noah Brooks.* Baltimore: Johns Hopkins University Press, c. 1998.

Cunnington, C. Willett. *English Women's Clothing in the Nineteenth Century.* New York: Dover Publications, Inc., c. 1990.

Durbin, Louise. *Inaugural Cavalcade.* New York: Dodd, Mead & Company, c. 1971.

Fales, Martha Grandy. *Jewelry in America: 1600–1900.* Woodbridge, Suffolk, UK: Antique Collector's Club, c. 1995.

Gernsheim, Alison. *Victorian and Edwardian Fashion: A Photographic Survey.* New York: Dover Publications, Inc., c. 1981.

Green, Harvey, and Mary Ellen Perry. *The Light of the Home: An Intimate View of the Lives of Women in Victorian America.* New York: Pantheon, c. 1983.

Hale, Sarah Josepha. *Early American Cookery: "The Good Housekeeper" 1841.* New York: Dover Publications Inc., c. 1996.

Hamilton, Charles, and Lloyd Ostendorf. *Lincoln in Photographs: An Album of Every Known Pose.* Dayton, Ohio: Morningside House Inc., c. 1985.

Helm, Katherine. *Mary, Wife of Lincoln.* New York: Harper Brothers. Publishing Co., c. 1928.

Holzer, Harold, Gabor S. Boritt, and Mark E. Neely, Jr. *The Lincoln Image: Abraham Lincoln and the Popular Print.* Champaign: University of Illinois Press, c. 2001.

Keckley, Elizabeth. *Behind the Scenes.* Salem, NH: Ayer Company Publishers, Inc., c. 1868, Reprint edition 1989.

Kunhardt, Dorothy Meserve, and Philip B. Kunhardt, Jr. *Twenty Days: A Narrative in Text and Pictures of the Assassination of Abraham Lincoln and the Twenty Days and Nights that followed – The Nation in Mourning, the Long Trip Home to Springfield.* Secaucus, NJ: Castle Books, 1993.

Kunhardt, Philip B. Jr., Philip B. Kunhardt III, and Peter W. Kunhardt. *Lincoln: An Illustrated Biography.* New York: Random House, c. 1992.

Loring, John. *Tiffany's 150 Years.* Garden City, NY: Doubleday, c. 1987.

Majka, Holly. *Life in the Midst of Death: A Victorian Manual for Mourning.* North Canton, OH: Golden Cord Clothiers, c. 1996.

Mehaffey, Karen Rae. *The After-Life: Mourning Rituals and the Mid-Victorians.* Pipestone, MN: Laser Writers Publishing, c. 1993.

Miers, Earl Schenck, ed. *Lincoln Day by Day: A Chronology 1809–1865.* Dayton, OH: Morningside, c. 1991.

Neely, Mark E. Jr., and R. Gerald McMurtry. *The Insanity File: The Case of Mary Todd Lincoln.* Carbondale, IL: Southern Illinois Press, c. 1986.

Nicolay, Helen. *Lincoln's Secretary: A Biography of John G. Nicolay.* New York: Longmans, Green, and Co., c. 1949.

Olian, Jo Anne. *80 Godey's Full-Color Fashion Plates 1838–1880.* New York: Dover Publications Inc., c. 1998.

Ostendorf, Lloyd. *The Photographs of Mary Todd Lincoln.* Springfield: The Illinois Historic Preservation Agency, c. 1989. Book reprinted from the Autumn 1968 *Journal of the Illinois State Historical Society.* Volume LXI, No. 3.

Randall, Ruth Painter. *Mary Lincoln, Biography of a Marriage.* Boston: Little Brown and Company, c. 1953.

Searcher, Victor. *Lincoln's Journey to Greatness.* Philadelphia: John Winston, c. 1960.

Shep, R. L. *Civil War Ladies: Fashions and Needle-Arts of the Early 1860's.* California: R. L. Shep, c. 1987.

Singleton, Esther. *The Story of the White House.* New York: The McClure Company, c. 1907.

Turner, Justin, and Linda Levitt Turner. *Mary Todd Lincoln: Her Life and Letters.* New York: Alfred A. Knopf, c. 1972.

Newspapers
Chicago Tribune. January 6, 1862, p. 1.

"Disgraceful." *The Conservative.* Clarksburg, WVa. November 9, 1867, col. 2.

Gordon, Beulah. "Coffee Spilled on Borrowed Nuptial Gown of Mary Todd." *Illinois State Journal.* August 16, 1942. The Lincoln Museum, Fort Wayne, IN.

"Grand Reception at the White House, January, 1862 – Sketched by Mr. A. Waud. *Harper's Weekly.* January 25, 1862, pp. 56–57.

Harper's Weekly newspaper. November 8, 1862, page 700, col. 1.

"Inauguration Ball At Washington On the 4th of March." *Frank Leslie's Illustrated Newspaper.* New York: March 23, 1861, No. 278, Volume XI, p. 285, col. 1.

"The Levee at the White House." *Chicago Tribune.* January 29, 1862. Front page, col. 3. www.pqasb.pqarchiver.com

Lexington, Kentucky Observer and Reporter. February 15, 1862.

"Mrs. Abraham Lincoln." *Chicago Tribune.* July 20, 1882, p. 3, col. 2.

"Mrs. Lincoln." *Wheeling Intelligencer.* Thursday, October 10, 1867, p. 1, col. 2.

"Mrs. Lincoln at Mount Washington," *Chicago Tribune.* August 14, 1863, p. 2. www.pqasb.pqarchiver.com.

"Mrs. Lincoln and her Wardrobe." *Chicago Tribune*, October 7, 1867, front page, col. 2.

"New Year's Reception at the White House." *Chicago Tribune.* January 9, 1864, Front page, col. 1. www.pqasb.pqarchiver.com

New York Herald. March 13, 1861

The New York Times. March 6, 1861; March 7, 1865; March 8, 1865. (ALPL)

New York World. March 5, 1861.

"News Paragraphs." *Chicago Tribune.* December 30, 1863, page 3. www.pqasb.pqarchiver.com

"The Presidential Party." *Frank Leslie's Illustrated Newspaper,* New York: February 22, 1862. No. 326, Vol. XIII, p. 209 cols. 1–3, and p. 213 cols. 2–3.

The State Journal-Register. May 3, 1976, p. 21.

Swisshelm, Jane Grey. "Tribute to the Dead." *Chicago Tribune.* July 20, 1882, p. 7.

Washington Chronicle. January 22, 1865.

Magazines and Journals

Grimsley, Elizabeth Todd. "Six Months in the White House." *Journal of the Illinois State Historical Society.* Springfield: Vol. XIX, October 1926–January 1927, Nos. 3–4, pp. 43–73.

Hirschhom, Nobert and Robert G. Feldman. "Mary Lincoln's Final Illness: A Medical and Historical Reappraisal." *Journal of the History of Medicine,* Vol. 54, October 1999.

James, Jeannie H., and Wayne C. Temple. "Mrs. Lincoln's Clothing." *Lincoln Herald,* Summer, 1960, pp. 54–65.

Kinnaid, Virginia. "Mrs. Lincoln as a White House Hostess." *Journal of the Illinois State Historical Society.* Springfield: Reprint from *Papers in Illinois History and Transactions for the Year 1938*, pp. 3–26.

Neely, Mark Jr., editor. "Mary Todd Lincoln (1818–1882)." *Lincoln Lore,*
Bulletin of the Lincoln Library and Museum, November 1981, No. 1725,
p. 1.

Ross, Rodney A. "Mary Todd Lincoln, Patient At Bellevue Place, Batavia."
Journal of the Illinois State Historical Society. Springfield: Spring 1970, pp.
5–34.

Letters and Manuscripts

Edwards, Elizabeth, to Julia Edwards Baker. March 2, 1862. Manuscript
Department, SC 445, ALPLM.

Helm, Emily Todd. Random notes from her wartime diary. Mary Townsend
Murphy Collection, private.

*Lincoln's Marriage: Newspaper Interview with Mrs. Frances Wallace, Springfield,
Illinois, September 2, 1895.* Privately Printed, 1917. Lincoln Collection,
ALPL.

Lincoln, Mary, to Dr. Willis Danforth. August 1874. Manuscript
Department, ALPL.

Norris, Elizabeth Humphreys, to Emily Todd Helm. September 28, 1895.
Manuscript Department, SC1980, ALPL.

Smith, Ann, to Emily Todd Helm. Letter, June 19 (no year, but believed to be
1881). Private (unnamed) collection.

Stuart, Emily Huntington. *Some Recollections of the Early Days in Springfield
and Reminiscences of Abraham Lincoln and Other Celebrities who Lived in
that Little Town in My Youth.* Illinois Society, DAR Genealogy Records,
1940–1941.

Miscellaneous

Holzer, Harold. Press Release for The Metropolitan Museum of Art. New
York, NY, May 22, 2000.

Smithsonian Institution, National Museum of American History, Division of
Politics & Reform, First Ladies Collection. Catalog file #241232.1.

Smithsonian Institution, National Museum of American History, Division of Politics & Reform, First Ladies' Collection. Catalog card #33280B.

Smithsonian Institution, National Museum of American History, Division of Politics & Reform, First Ladies' Collection. Catalog card #33280D.

Verdict of the Jury, May 19, 1875. Chicago Historical Society. Lincoln Collection, 1876, Box 236, Folder 306.

Index